Seasons of the Feminine Divine

CYCLE A

Seasons of the Feminine Divine

*Christian Feminist Prayers
for the Liturgical Cycle*

CYCLE A

— ℘ —

MARY KATHLEEN SPEEGLE SCHMITT

CROSSROAD • NEW YORK

1995

The Crossroad Publishing Company
370 Lexington Avenue, New York, NY 10017

Copyright © 1995 by Mary Kathleen Speegle Schmitt

Printed in the United States of America

Library of Congress Cataloging-in-Publication Data
(Revised for vol. 3)

Schmitt, Mary Kathleen Speegle.
    Seasons of the feminine divine : Christian feminist prayers for the liturgical cycle / Mary Kathleen Speegle Schmitt.
        p.   cm.
    Vol. [3] based on Cycle A of the Common lectionary.
    Includes bibliographical references and index.

    Contents : [1. Without special title] [2 Cycle C] [3] Cycle A.

    ISBN 0-8245-1515-3 (v. 3)
    1. Church year—Prayer-books and devotions—English. 2. Women—Religious life. I. Title.

BV30.S323 1995
264'.13'092—dc20   93-588
                                                                   CIP

For my cousins

CAROLYN AND SUZANNE,

Soul-sisters of my childhood

Contents

— ∾ —

Prayers after Pentecost:
Womangod as Matriarch **97**
Sundays in Ordinary Time, June 19–August 6

Introduction

In prayer we draw near to the divine, an action both audacious and natural. Prayer is audacious because we presume that mere creatures of limited time and space may open conversation with a Being who is infinite and without limitation except that expressly chosen. Prayer is natural because we are turning to the One who is the Source of our existence. We turn to her as a child to its mother, without fear because we know in our very bones that She desires and loves us. In one sense we hesitate: how do we address the Holy One? Is there one appropriate name? Can any one name be adequate for a Being described in one Hebrew tradition as a cloud four miles long? Or a Being far beyond the reaches of the keenest human imagination?

The Hebrew Quest to Know the Divine

Until Moses' time, the Divine would not reveal his/her[1] name. Some have suggested that for Yahweh to give a name is synonymous with giving the person addressing the Divine power over the Divine. It does not seem possible to me that a human being can have power over the Divine. More likely, as human beings we imagine that we have such a power, which results in a distortion in the Divine–human relationship.

So the people of Hebrew times did not pronounce the name "Yahweh"—an elusive name in itself. Biblical scholars over the ages have speculated on its meaning, the closest rendition of which in my understanding is "Being," a reality that is vast and beyond human understanding. At the same time, the Hebrew people did find substitutes for the name of the Divine, translated in English as "Lord" and "Almighty God," "Rock," "Shepherd," "Creator" or "Maker," and others. There had to be some way to talk about the Divine, even though the people clearly understood that the totality of "Yahweh"—and perhaps even the essence of the Divine—was beyond human comprehension.

Language and the Naming of the Divine

It is certain that the people using names such as "Shepherd" or "Rock" did not think of Yahweh as literally a shepherd or rock. Biblical writers quote Yahweh as saying repeatedly that the Divine is not limited to something or someone physical. In the historical books the prophets ridiculed the people who worshiped the wood statues to Asherah. The implication was that adherents of Asherah believed that the statues were in reality Asherah rather than symbols or representations of Asherah or other gods and goddesses.[2] Idolaters at best were accused of being simple-minded.

It is difficult for the modern mind to comprehend the metaphorical way that language was used before the Age of Reason. The current emphasis on empirical, scientific definitions leaves our language stripped of almost anything beyond a literal understanding of a word. This poverty of language results in a multitude of distortions in the Church. The large majority of Christians today experience confusion because of their literal mode of understanding. The resulting narrow interpretations rob the Bible of its evocative power to speak beyond legalisms to deeper truths.

The work of Sally McFague and others offers us a way to move out of the impasse of literal biblical interpretation through regaining a sense of the symbolic nature of language. She suggests that the Bible leads the Church to encounter the Divine in metaphors of aspects of creation,[3] for instance,

Rock; Devouring Fire; Eagle; Bear; Lover; Still, Small Voice; Dove; Father; and Christ. Metaphors are literary devices that have enabled people both ancient and modern to express deep meaning with images of concrete objects, beings, perceptions, and feelings. Metaphorical thinking involves intuitive, creative thinking and is intended to expand our understanding beyond the image itself to a deeper meaning. Metaphors are never intended to be used as analytical definition. Yahweh is not a rock or an eagle, yet the images of rock or eagle can communicate some truth about Yahweh. By joining concepts and experiences that may not seem to be related, it is possible to discover new insights about the Divine.[4]

The Bible, therefore, witnesses to the complexity of the Divine, a deity who cannot be captured in any written word, yet who comes to us even in an image as simple as a wildflower or a sparrow. To believe, however, that the Divine is literally a bird or a piece of grass would verge on the ridiculous. These images have power because they are not literal. They are metaphors and can resonate within the heart of each person who reads the word and lives into the words with passion and imagination. To limit understanding of the Divine to a literal biblical text would be impoverishing and would rob the Church of a living relationship with the Divine, who comes not only in the Bible but through every facet of life. The Bible sets the chosen people on a journey and guides that journey in the context of the church community.

The name "Father" for the Divine is a metaphor. Just as "Father" emerged in the prophetic times as an appropriate way to address the Divine and was taken up by Jesus—"Abba, Father"— as a means of expressing a dimension of Divine Love that few people before that time could discern, so feminist Christians reach back into the stores of Judeo-Christian tradition to find names that express an understanding of the Divine that is emerging in our own time. For Jesus, the use of the title "Father" was a recognition of a relational tenderness as compared to the concept of the

Divine as a judgmental deity who must be appeased. The writings of the early Church attest to the joy that this new understanding of Yahweh brought to the people, Jew and Gentile alike, who could hear Jesus' message of Divine Love.

Justice and Female Metaphor for the Divine

Incredible among the implications of this good news was a new inclusiveness. Jewish Christians no longer turned away from associating with other peoples, such as Samaritans and Gentiles. In the early Christian movement there was also a strong move to include women in the leadership roles of congregations, and there is evidence that in some Christian communities the title "Mother" was used for the Holy.[5] These phenomena were short-lived, however, as Christianity became the established religion of the Roman Empire and it became important in the minds of some of its leaders to regularize the church community according to the norm of Roman society, in which women had secondary roles.[6] However, out of the faith and discernment of the Christian community, new levels of understanding were developed concerning divine justice—for instance, the formation of hospitals, the opening of orphanages, care for the infirm and mentally ill, the giving of relief to the poor, the abolition of slavery, public education, the bringing of justice and relief for workers, and eventually the demand that secular government take responsibility for the vulnerable ones of the society. Like these other justice movements, Christian feminism arises from the heart of divine justice evident in the revolutionary actions and teachings of Jesus. Because of Jesus' respect for women in the gospel stories, there have been Christians through the ages who, despite the conventions of their times, have discerned the dignity of women in the image of Yahweh and have found the courage to proclaim in both church and world what the Holy Spirit was saying to them through scripture.

Today, in the context of a worldview that includes the evolution of creation, we understand that our knowledge of the Holy is evolving as, layer by layer, we comprehend the impact of human cruelty upon human community, and we repent and allow Divine Love to grow more richly within us. While the issues of the equality and dignity of women and of the poor are among those that are current both in church and society, undoubtedly there are issues that today some of us think a little bizarre—such as animal rights—that will become the issues of justice for tomorrow, as our consciousness of our interconnectedness with all of creation grows.

When feminist Christians reach back into the storehouse of tradition to bring forth names such as Mother, Midwife, Womb, Shekinah (numinous feminine presence), Shaddai (deity with breasts), Sophia (Divine Wisdom), and the understanding of Holy Spirit as feminine, they do so out of new insight into the nature of the Gospel that has implications for the order and language of the Church today as in every age. There is no suggestion, however, that understanding, portraying, or addressing the Divine in the feminine is the only way of relating to the Divine. This exploration is only part of the quest in the Christian community to follow the vision of wholeness given us by Christ. The prayers in this book offer one possibility of moving this exploration around justice for women and an understanding of the feminine dimension of the Divine from the intellectual realm into practice. Through a narrative and poetic approach our relationship with the Divine can be opened up and expanded. Through repetition of images over time, this new apprehension of the Divine has the possibility of moving from the intellectual level to the deepest part of our souls.

The Female Divine and Creation

The return to human consciousness of the Divine Feminine is also a return to a standard against which Hebrew religion originally defined itself: the high value of creation not as a resource for human consumption or a territory to conquer nor a wild thing to bring under control, but for its own intrinsic goodness. The concrete, physical reality of nature is good. Human beings as part of this creation are intrinsically good.

Our bodies, for all their limitations and vulnerability, are good. Our sexual natures are good.[7]

This value for creation, while expressed in limited and covert ways in Judeo-Christian tradition, is a big shift in our understanding of the Divine–human relationship. As the male-centered nature of the Hebrew religion emerged in vivid contrast to the female nature cycle and fertility emphases of ancient Goddess religion, nature became regarded as alien, bodies (especially female bodies) were deemed inferior to thought and spirit, and female sexuality was viewed as something dangerous but necessary that had to be contained and controlled.

The theology that developed suggested that the link between the Divine and creation was broken. Human nature was depraved and needed to be redeemed. Nature, although understood as created by the Holy One, was suspect. The type of wisdom that had in the past been valued was now devalued. The great religion that had once been known through the regenerative symbol of serpent was squarely identified as the source of evil. The Divine was seen as "out there" rather than within creation. The new religion systematically attacked and devalued the old values over thousands of years until the dualistic split in human understanding was complete. A major consequence of this movement was the splitting off of religious experience from sexual experience that had been central both to understanding and ritual in ancient times.

Yet with the coming of Christ, a bridge was made between the Spirit and creation. The Divine entered—and did not despise!—the human body of Mary, was born as Jesus Christ, and lived and died as did other humans. At Pentecost the Holy Spirit entered into Jesus' disciples or at least became recognized as present by them. Human beings became the Body of Christ—the embodiment of the Holy. Although physically limited and vulnerable, our bodies house the Divine Presence. The prologue of John's Gospel goes a step beyond humanity to the role of Christ as Wisdom's activity in the creation of the universe. So it is not human bodies only that house the Sacred; the Universe itself is the Body of God.[8] In revaluing the Divine Feminine, we are in a process of healing the dualistic split between body and soul, mind and matter, male and female, and so on. Heaven is no longer "out there" or beyond creation. In fact, the Aramaic word we translate as "heaven" actually means "universe" as "experienced through word or vibration."[9] The Divine chooses to live within the temporal body of the Universe. The Divine chooses to live within each of us. This is not a relationship of sacred and profane in the sense of one being of greater value than the other, but of incredible interconnection with us chosen by the Holy. Body and creation are not inferior and do not contaminate. Even the female body that has been objectified as evil for so long is liberated, as we hear in Mary's song of thanksgiving, the Magnificat.

This belief in the presence of the Divine within us, the Pauline "Christ in us," began the deep healing necessary to bring humankind back in touch with the value and goodness of creation, and our joy in our bodies as that which houses the Holy One. By redeeming the feminine dimension of the Divine, the connection between the Holy One and creation, we are restored to our bodies and the goodness of bodily existence. We gain the possibility of experiencing healing. We rediscover our deep connection to creation and value other creatures and all the universe as we value our bodies, with sensitivity and care. Virginia Mollenkott would describe this experience as recognizing that the Divine Stream of Consciousness flows through all of creation, and that "I am a sinless Self traveling through eternity and temporarily having human experiences in a body."[10] Many of the images in Seasons of the Feminine Divine draw upon images from nature and from human experience, because we recognize the link between our experience as part of creation and our experience of the Divine.

The Role of Eros in Divine–Human Relationship

In patriarchal religious tradition humankind came into relationship with the Divine through intellect, abstract thought, and eventually in the ascetic movement, spirit.[11] Already in considerable disrepute, sensuality as a door to spirituality was obliterated by Augustine, Bishop of Hippo, at the Council of Elvira in 381 C.E. The attitude toward sexuality that followed has been described as erotophobia "as a staple of Christian orthodoxy."[12] In contrast to the patriarchal approach, Phyllis Trible suggests that eros or desire is actually closer to the love between humankind and the Divine as described in the Bible than is the traditionally used word *agape*, which is a love that is, in a sense, disinterested—a benevolent trustee as compared to a lover. For instance, the picture of Divine Love in the Song of Songs is intensely erotic. Without our longing for the Holy One we might not even seek the Divine.[13] Mollenkott, too, speaks of eros as "a spiritual urge"[14] and refers to Schopenhauer's belief that sexual passion is "the kernel of the will to live," or at least "one primary indicator of the will to live."[15] A biblical corollary may be seen in the Johannine epistles in which the will toward light and life are synonymous with the will to be one with the Divine.

Humankind, because of its need for fulfillment and relationship, is created for community, and ultimately is drawn into intimacy with the Holy. Eros is that need or desire or passion that draws us together despite fear, despite past wounds and brokenness, and despite our best defenses.[16] Carter Heyward describes the erotic as "our most fully embodied experience of the love of God" and the "source of our capacity for transcendence, crossing over, and making connections between ourselves in relationship."[17] Yet humans are not the only ones to experience longing. The book of Hosea gives a vivid picture of the Divine as desiring humankind and longing to be in reciprocal relationship. Julian of Norwich wrote that "God is thirsty for everyone. This thirst has already drawn the

Holy to Joy and the living are ever being drawn and drunk. And yet God still thirsts and longs."[18] Eros calls us into the journey and into the numinous sphere of Goddess' yearning to be united with us in love.

The image of the Divine as exotic dancer in the prayer "Woman of Rhythm" seeks to reconnect us with the passion and beauty of the sensuous Feminine from which we as women of faith have been denied for centuries. To image the Sacred One with her connection to human—and female—sexuality is to begin to remove the taboo imposed by centuries of tradition. Because the Feminine Divine delights in the sensuous, women are given permission to delight in their own bodily experience as again in the image of the Holy and to move toward the healing of their self-hatred as persons who are subordinate in the social structure. As we are restored to our sense of bodily goodness, we are also restored to the value of all bodies, female and male, of all races and sexual orientations, and to the universe, the Body of the Divine.

The Divine Circle: Journey to Sophia

As we continue to live in encounter with the Divine, ourselves, and others around the cycle of the seasons, we are journeying toward Wisdom or Sophia. The seasons give a rhythm and an order to this passage through life, blending our inner and outer worlds and bringing us to consciousness. This worldly excursion is always circular, beginning with our conception and life in the womb of the Mother, and ending with our return to wholeness in Her. In our travels we make an inner voyage across the dark, rolling sea of unknowing. We also explore the outer world of human community and the sensuous terrain of the creation. Our well-being varies along this trip. We suffer from attacks, injuries, and mistakes. We find the treasures of healing, compassion, and passion that enable our move toward wholeness and our arrival in the end at home.

How This Volume of Seasons Relates
to the First Two Volumes

This volume of *Seasons of the Feminine Divine* is the third in
a trilogy of prayer cycles based on the ecumenical lectionary.
These prayers relate to Sunday readings of the Revised
Common, Episcopal, Lutheran, Roman Catholic, and
Anglican Church of Canada lectionaries. The prayers in this
book relate to Cycle A.

For further information regarding the reasons for seeking
out the Feminine Divine, the ways She has been present
throughout Judeo-Christian tradition, the relationship of
ancient Goddess religion to Judeo-Christian tradition, the problem posed by the maleness of Jesus for women of faith, and the
narrative and poetic nature of the prayers in these cycles, see
Volume B (1993). For a deeper examination of issues around
the association of gender with our understanding of the Divine,
the use of repetition in prayer images, the problem of stereo-
typing, and the importance of cyclical worship in spiritual formation, see Volume C (1994). In this volume (A) I discuss the
emergence of our understanding of justice, and the relationship
of ecological justice to justice for women.

Suggestions for Using These Prayers in the Local Congregation

W HEN I FIRST WROTE THESE PRAYERS, I thought that most likely they would be used by women's groups and in private devotions, and it has been a great joy to me to hear the prayers read in a variety of situations, and to hear reports of people who have used them for their own Lenten devotionals, and in other personal prayer. Certainly I had found them very helpful in enabling both women and men to expand their consciousness of the Divine as I provided spiritual direction and facilitated weeklong summer courses related to the themes of *Seasons*.

When I discovered that, from time to time, some of the prayers were being used in congregations, I was even more pleased, because it seems to me that the Spirit is moving in opening our hearts as the people of the Christian community to a wonderful new dimension of faith and relationship with the Divine. Now I am receiving inquiries concerning the implementation of these prayers in congregations and requests for assistance in doing so.

In the first volume of *Seasons*, I advised that it is important to provide preparation before using prayers addressing or portraying the Divine in the feminine in a congregational (or other) setting. Preparation does not guarantee that there will not be some strong adverse reactions to the use of female language and imagery, but so be it—a strong adverse reaction is often the beginning of someone's journey to discover the Holy in a new way, and it is important for us to allow people their particular journeys and not to be afraid of those journeys. At the same time, pain is not the only way for people to grow, and if we can open the way to understanding and moving into the presence of the Holy One in a new dimension in the way of unfolding consciousness, gently and in small steps, we empower people rather than overwhelm them or give them a sense of being overpowered.

My approach to working in parishes in terms of language issues has been threefold: exploration of inclusive language as it relates to women's role and identity and to justice issues pertaining to women; exploration of metaphorical thinking and metaphors for the Divine; and exploration of the Divine as female. Obviously, needs vary from congregation to congregation. Some congregations may have done extensive work on inclusive language but not on female metaphors for the Divine, and would therefore need to start with the second phase.

Gender in God-language makes no sense to people if they do not understand the justice issues underlying the move to include female language for the Divine. Until we recognize that there is a correspondence between the Church's attitudes and actions toward women and the abuse of women, the limiting of women in their roles in the community, and the low self-esteem of women with all of the consequences of lack of dignity, we will not understand the issue of the gender of the Divine. Unless we grasp the metaphorical nature of the Bible and of names of the Divine, and see that even such an all-pervasive title for the Divine as "Father" is metaphorical and not literal, we will not appreciate the need to incorporate other names, especially feminine titles, into the reality of day-to-day worship. Being cognizant of the long history of the presence of the female dimension of the Divine in Judeo-Christian tradition, therefore, assists us as we seek out ways of expressing our recognition of this aspect of our relationship with the Holy.

It is helpful, as well, to identify the way life is ordered in a particular community. In some congregations, study groups or retreats which include personal reflection, discussion, the sharing of stories, and prayer might be the place to begin to create awareness of some of these issues which then filter into the mainstream of the community life. In others, the starting place would be the worship or liturgy committee, moving through a process of study which includes the three aspects of inclusivity and justice, metaphorical thinking, and female images for the Divine. Such processes can be supported through sermons if the preacher is open to the idea. From these beginnings, it may be important to introduce these same concepts to the parish council or congregational board or session, with a view to coming to a consensus or decision to make a commitment to introduce female imagery or language into the worship service. Again, the congregation as a whole then needs to move through the same process of reflection on the justice issues, the nature of language, exploration of female Divine Presence in Judeo-Christian tradition, and ways female or feminine images are beneficial to us today in our proclamation of the Gospel.

Key to the process are the personal integrity of the facilitators, a willingness to allow individuals to be where they are on the issues being explored, and an openness to the work of the Holy Spirit in the lives of these people. It means leaving behind assumptions such as "It will be the older people who resist hearing what is being said" (often not true!), and finding a way to constructively be with people who find the whole process alien or uncomfortable or frightening.

In some denominational groups, members approach issues more intellectually than others. My experience in the context of the Anglican Church of Canada has been that a low-key, personal approach is more likely to communicate than an adversarial tack. My observation of congregations of various denominations that have proceeded in an adversarial manner is that division and bitterness are almost inevitably the result. This does not at all suggest that we do not proceed in the face of opposition or resistance, or that our worship should represent the lowest possible common denominator of dis-ease.

What we are concerned about is justice for groups and individuals; the ideology is there, but it is in the background. The focus is always on people and their spiritual growth as the Holy Spirit works in their hearts and minds and in our own. As Letty Russell has pointed out, we are partners working with the Divine; even for those of us who feel we are down the road in front of others in a particular aspect of spiritual formation, we walk a step at a time, testing ourselves, our own understanding, receiving challenges humbly and reflectively, and looking always for Wisdom to make herself known in the midst of the community.

Introducing gender issues of the Divine into a congregation is not just a trend or diversion. It is a long-term commitment which involves courage, hope, frustration, anger, disappointment, joy, love, and always perseverence.

Whether you are working within a congregational community or are making this journey on your own, I pray for you courage and wisdom and the blessing of the discovery of soul-sisters and -brothers. May the love of the Shekinah surround you and permeate your very being; may the breasts of Shaddai feed and sustain you; may you receive discernment and sensitivity and a deeper compassion from the hands and heart of Divine Wisdom; and may Ruah carry you in the flow of her love forever.

The Prayers

The Season of Advent

—— ❧ ——

A SEASON OF DARKNESS, Advent is a time of going within ourselves. This entering into the darkness of our unconscious life may be caused by a crisis, a life transition, a spiritual shift, or simply by the grayness of the onset of winter. The darkness is that of the Divine Womb; we remember our time in the uterus of our earth-mother and reflect. Sometimes it is necessary to grieve for who our mother was, for who she could not be for us, for her woundedness and our own. We know eros in the need of our cells for nourishment and in our constant listening to the common beating of our mother's heart.

Yet in the womb of the Divine Mother we experience darkness as nourishing and nurturing. Encompassed within her, we experience unimpeded, unconditional love that results in a profound sense of safety and peace. The peace that is possible within the Great Mother is of a different order from what we experienced in the uteruses of our human mothers, no matter how loving they were. We perceive the Mother as our Universe, that Body that contains us. We imagine her to be all-powerful and all-knowing, and having all power over us, but She does not exert her power as power over. She is Judge; yet She is neither arbitrary nor partial. In her gentleness She seeks justice for each of us, and as Weaver creates justice for us all in the tapestry of the New Creation. She is the Blossom that makes the wasteland beautiful. No matter how often the movement of her creativity is cut off, the Vine of her love rises again and again. Complete within herself, She is true Virgin, Mother-Child-and-Holy Spirit, Goddess all-in-all, from

whom we draw the breath of life and in whom, through
Christ, is our hope.

Advent 1

WOMANJUDGE

- "Then [Yahweh] will judge between the nations and arbitrate
  between many peoples. They will hammer their swords into
  ploughshares and their spears into sickles. . . . No longer will
  they learn how to make war." (Isaiah 2:4, NJB)

- Womanjudge,
    your gentleness takes away our fear,
    and your passion for justice
        awakens us to hope.
    Dismantle within us the hatred
    that makes us enemies of one another
        and of this earth:
    that, caught up in the impartiality
        of your love,
    we discover our unity with You
        and all creation;
    One Who Listens,
    One Who Hears,
    Spirit Who Transforms the Universe.
    Amen.

LAMENT ON THE ENMITY OF PEOPLES

- Weaver of the Universe,
    war erupts about us in every direction,
    and when one battle is resolved, another begins!
    Young women and men are raped and killed;
    their bodies melted, poisoned, shattered, and obliterated.
    Many of those who survive are left maimed,
        embittered, or in perpetual shock.
    The old woman carrying her basket to the market,

the grandfather leaning on his cane as he takes
    his morning walk,
children playing hide-and-seek among the trees
    in the school yard:
all are wiped out in an instant to achieve
    some military objective.
Peoples are duped with lies about the enemy,
stories of atrocities that never happened,
infants murdered in their incubators,
so that we support the taking of human lives—
so long as the casualties are "theirs" and not "ours."
The poor, filled with the idealism of patriotism,
cast themselves before the armies of devouring empires;
they are martyred for the sakes of the wealthy and
    powerful.
Governments spend billions to put on a show of force
    to garner votes,
while thousands languish in poverty in the very streets
    of their capitals.
Citizens who could work to turn the tide
    of ecological devastation
labor for munitions factories, turning out instruments
    of slaughter.
We cry "peace, peace!" but there is no peace!

Holy One, are You not the Author of Justice?
How can You permit the continuation of the devastation
    of humankind,
this destruction that ravages the earth
and makes our planet into a wasteland
    where no thing can live?
Turn back to us with your wisdom
    that is partial to no one,
with your cherishing that refuses to discriminate,
with your truth that claims every person to be of value.
Give us the will to love our enemies:
that we not yield to the temptation to hate others

but learn to use our anger wisely.
Thread the loom of your cosmos with loving kindness,
sending the shuttle of your peace throughout the world,
and with patience unravel the tangles of human
    contentiousness;
that we weave with You the tapestry of the new creation,
    world without end. Amen.

Advent 2

FLOURISHING VINE

- "A shoot will spring from the stock of Jesse, a new shoot will grow from his roots. On him will rest the spirit of Yahweh, the spirit of wisdom . . . insight . . . counsel . . . power . . ." (Isaiah 11:1–2, NJB)

   ❧ Flourishing Vine,
       even though You are cut off
       from the face of the earth,
       your roots will not die.
       You sprout forth again and again
       from the soil You have nourished
           with your presence.
       Bring to blossom from the depths
           of our hearts
       the flowering of your Divine Love:
       that, filled with the flow
           of your compassion,
       we bring your beauty to the world;
       Hope of Wisdom,
       Prophetic Word,
       You are Motherly Compassion.[19] Amen.

Advent 3

GODDESS AS DESERT BLOSSOM

- "Let the desert and the dry lands be glad, let the wasteland rejoice and bloom; like the asphodel, let it burst into flower." (Isaiah 35:1–2, NJB)

🙊 Desert Blossom,
   You call to us in the dry places
      of our bodies and souls.
   Tickle our noses with the spiciness
      of your scent:
   that, sustained by the juiciness
      of your thick leaves,
   we awake to your promise of new life.
   Rose of the Cosmos,
   Sweet Briar,
   You are the Morning-Glory
      that climbs to meet the sun!
   Amen.

Advent 4

VIRGIN GODDESS

- "The Lord will give you a sign. . . . The young woman is with child and will give birth to a son whom she will call Immanuel." (Isaiah 7:14, NJB)

- The title "Virgin" is broader than the restrictive definition understood in Christian tradition that emphasized the woman's not having had sexual intercourse. In Goddess religions, the title had to do with the totality of woman's life cycle—woman's role as uninitiated girl, as mother, as post-menopausal woman—so that the emphasis was on her completeness in herself without

dependence on others. From this perspective, there is no con-
tradiction between being virginal—uninitiated—and being a
mother, as has been experienced by many women in Christian
tradition.[20] Both aspects of our womanness are part of the
whole, which is entitled "virginity."

• Hadewijch of Brabant, writing on chastity or virginity, said
  "For love is always discovering and teaching and consuming
  within herself. And yet she is complete within herself. . . . And
  yet nothing sustains Love herself but her own wholeness."[21]

   ❧ Virgin Goddess,
      complete within your Self,
      You yet desire to be One
      with all that You have created.
      From the depths of your belly
      speak to us of your love:
      that, made new by the knowledge
      of your great regard for us,
      we seek to nurture every element
         of this earth.
      Birth-Giving Mother,
      Awakening Child,
      the flow of your compassion
      is the consummation of the Universe.
      Amen.

The Season of Christmas

IN CHRISTMAS WE ARE BORN ANEW INTO THE WORLD. Our passage through the birth canal is vigorous and rhythmic and healthy. Birth from the Divine Mother can only be perfect. We do not experience fear or pain. In the very instant that we experience the shock of the light of day, we are in her arms. For the first time we see the beauty of her face as She smiles down upon us, weary with the effort of her creativity but joyous at the creation She has made us to be. Though the umbilical cord is cut, our connection to her remains deep and unsevered.

Yet there is another sense in which it is all very different. Although in her, we are also born from our earthly mothers whose love and anger, hopes and fears, acceptance and rejection we have incorporated into our bodies. There is still the sense of safety and trust, but it is partial because we take part in the human condition. The peace that we long for continues to elude us. As Midwife, Sophia guides and protects us through the channel of emotional birth into the mist of the morning. Startled by the light, the circle of faces peering at us, the noise, and the hands touching us gently, we are momentarily disoriented. Eros makes her appearance as we drift slowly towards awareness of our vulnerability. We delight in the tightness of our swaddling bands. We long for the embrace of our Mother's arms. We hunger for the milk of her breasts.

Christmas Eve

DIVINE MOTHER

❧ Divine Mother,
out of your Womb of Night
You gave birth to Love
that transforms all creation.
Awaken us to your delight
    in each of us:
that, filled with the energy
    of your splendor,
we become ambassadors
    of your graciousness.
One Who Nourishes Us,
Love-Child,
You are Wisdom's Stream of Glory,
Womangod All-in-All. Amen.

LAMENT ON WOMEN IN POVERTY

❧ How long, Mother of All,
will your daughters be cast into the darkness of poverty,
left alone to survive without the resources to care for
    their children?
How long will these little ones, if they go to school at all,
    go without breakfast,
to come home to an empty room or to stay with
    loveless strangers?
How long will You allow their grandmothers to be cast
into the streets to wander with their garbage bags,
their beat-up shopping carts, rusted from days and
    nights of exposure to the elements,
parked near the doorway where their owners curl up
    to sleep on concrete,
huddling against cold rock to warm their old bones?

How much longer will your daughters sit on curbsides,
their hands stretched out in supplication,
their voices bleeding with sorrow
in the hope of receiving a few cents to tide them over
    one more day?
How long will women creep in pre-morning gloom
    to cross the bridge to a foreign city
where they work in the homes of the wealthy
for less than the children they care for receive
    for their weekly spending money?
How long must they sew for no money,
hunched over their pedal-driven machines
    in rooms with inadequate light,
wearing out their eyes to live in blindness in their old age?
The woman who peddles papayas in the village
    restaurant,
even yet is shooed into the streets, ignored, unheard
    and unpaid.

O Poorest of the Poor, You yourself lived in poverty
and knew the weight of the oppression of your people!
You had compassion for the widows and the orphans,
and gave your life for the cause of justice for those in need.
You raised from death the son of the widow of Nain
so that she might have comfort and support.
You cared for your widowed mother and at the
    time of your death
sought protection for her in the home of your
    beloved disciple.

Have compassion, then, on all who are poor!
Prevent us from judgment or contempt!
Enable us to look beyond the satisfactions we manage
    for ourselves to the vulnerability of our very being.
Teach us to live with less in order that the poor have more.

Let us be the vehicles of your desire to empower all
    who must depend upon others for their subsistence;
make us enablers of their journey to dignity and self-
    reliance.
For You, Mother, have given birth to everything that is;
You are the Breadmaker of the World;
and your Spirit longs to bring each of your children
    to the warmth of your hearth,
and to the nourishment of the banquet You have
    prepared for us in the Land of the Living, world
    without end.
Amen.

GODDESS[22] IN MARY

• "In that region there were shepherds living in the fields, keep-
ing watch over their flocks by night. Then an angel of the Lord
stood before them, and the glory of the Lord shone around
them." (Luke 2:8–9, NRSV)

🙠 Mother of All,
in the holy darkness of Mary's womb
You tamed wild Love
and gave us a lamb for the lion[23]
    of our previous experience.
Bestow the gift of your Divine Child
    in our hearts today:
that, illumined by your peace within us,
we become bearers of your Light
    in the depths of this blessed night.
Great Ancestress,
Fierce Protector,
You are the Christ-Spirit
who leads us into kinship with You.
Amen.

Christmas Day

WOMANJUDGE

- "[The Lord] will judge the peoples with equity." (Psalm 96:10, NRSV)

- "For the yoke of their burden . . . the rod of their oppressor, you have broken." (Isaiah 9:4, NRSV)

- "'Do not be afraid; for see—I am bringing you good news of great joy for all people.'" (Luke 2:10, NRSV)

    ❧ Womanjudge,
       your response to human sin
          is compassion,
       and your verdict the prescription
          of Love
       that removes fear of punishment.
       Bring to birth in us
       the Light of your saving goodness:
       that, made one with Christ,
       we become lamps along the pathway
          to your Shalom.
       Great Mother,
       Newborn Child,
       You are Love Love-Self,
       Eternal and Undivided Trinity. Amen.

Christmas 1

HOLY CHILD

- "Now after [the magi] had left, an angel of the Lord appeared to Joseph in a dream and said, 'Get up, take the child and his mother, and flee to Egypt . . . for Herod is about to search for the child, to destroy him.'" (Matthew 2:13, NRSV)

    ʕ Holy Child,
      in becoming fully human
      You accepted the dangers of mortality,
      and from the moment You touched earth
      were stalked by the powers of evil.
      In these times of uncertainty and violence,
      be present in our vulnerability:
      that, strengthened by Christ-in-us,
      we move with courage into the future.
      One Who Broods over Her Young,
      Cry of Rachel,
      You are our Advocate and Sustainer.
      Amen.

Christmas 2

BIRTH-GIVING MOTHER

- "Blessed be the God and Father of our Lord Jesus Christ, who has blessed us in Christ with every spiritual blessing in the heavenly places, just as he chose us in Christ before the foundation of the world to be holy and blameless before him in love." (Ephesians 1:3–5, NRSV)

- "In the beginning was the Word, and the Word was with God, and the Word was God." (John 1:1, NRSV)

- The title "Word" for Jesus was derived from the Hebrew "Wisdom," considered to be female in identity.

ॐ Birth-giving Mother,
    You imagined us long before
        we were conceived,
    and each of us is the apple
        of your eye.
    Fill us with the Wisdom
        of your everlasting Love:
    that, transformed by your radiance,
    we love You back with all our hearts
        and minds and souls;
    Intelligence of the Ages,
    Dancing, Laughing One,
    You are Joy personified. Amen.

The Season of Epiphany

IN EPIPHANY, GODDESS CALLS US FROM THE INNOCENCE of our infancy to explore the cosmos. Instinctively we know ourselves as part of that world and begin to have an inkling of our own inner process. Eros comes to us in our need for love and attention and our desire for playmates and pleasure. Wisdom's Star lights our path to the birth of infant Love in our hearts[24] and beckons us to new possibility. Goddess comes to us as the Sunbeam of Glory who scampers across our path and entrances us. She is the One who carries us when we hurt or are weary. In her we grow in wisdom and favor. We begin to learn that fairness does not always happen, but that justice is what we seek for ourselves and others. Like a clown, Sophia entices us along the pathway of Love and into the dance of the ongoing creation.

General

SHEKINAH

- "Arise, shine out, for your light has come, and the glory of Yahweh has risen on you. . . . Though night still covers the earth . . . on you Yahweh is rising and . . . his glory can be seen." (Isaiah 60:1–2, NJB)

- Sunbeam of Glory,
  You dance through the windows of our hearts
  to reveal your Presence in and with us.
  Cast the light of your healing across this earth:

that, illumined by your compassion,
humanity shines forth in love for You
    and one another;
Splendor of the Angels,
One Who Journeys with Us,
You are the Dawn of Our Heart's Desire. Amen.

BEARER OF THE WOUNDED ONES

❧ Bearer of the Wounded Ones,
as a mother carries her child on her hip,
You transport us from the exile
of human suffering and grief.[25]
Touch our imaginations with the vision
    of Shalom,
rich with loving-kindness:
that, encouraged by your promises,
we grow radiant with the fullness
    of your Love.
Mother of the Lost,
One Who Restores Us to Wholeness,
You are our Comforter. Amen.

The Feast of the Epiphany

WISDOM OF THE UNIVERSE

• "In the time of King Herod, after Jesus was born in Bethlehem of Judea, [Astrologers or Magi] from the East came to Jerusalem, asking, 'Where is the child . . . ?'" (Matthew 2:1–2, NRSV)

• Magi were "a class of Zoroastrian priests in ancient Media and Persia, reputed to possess supernatural powers."[26]

• The word for a sage or wise person comes from the root word sapi, meaning "taste." An old meaning of "sagacious" was "one keen of scent." The perennial herb, sage, used to season foods, was medicinal, as was sagebrush in North America, although the Latin roots of the two "sages" differ. The Norwegian saga, story of a person or family, was undoubtedly the wisdom handed down by the ancestors through the generations.[27]

> ⅌ Wisdom of the Universe,
>   with the brightness of a single star
>   You awakened the imaginations of the sages
>   as they scanned the heavens for the secret
>   of eternal life.
>   Reveal to us Christ-within-us:
>   that, tasting the empowerment of your
>   salvation,
>   we become beacons of your love to the world.
>   Saga of El Shaddai, Medicine Woman,
>   You are the Perennial Herb that brings us
>   to healing!
>   Amen.

STAR OF NIGHT

- "'Where is the child who has been born king of the Jews? For we observed his star at its rising, and have come to pay him homage.'" (Matthew 2:2, NRSV)

> ⅌ Star of Night,
>   when You announced the coming to earth
>   of the Divine Child,
>   You unlocked the Wisdom of the ages
>   and gave astrologers the key to the Universe.
>   Beckon us like them to follow You:
>   that, discovering ourselves in Christ,
>   we give our lives to your Glory forever.

> Luminous Body, Light of the Galaxies,
> the warmth of your Blaze draws all things
> into one! Amen.

Epiphany 1

HEAVENLY DOVE

- "... when Jesus ... came up from the water, ... the heavens
  ... opened to him and he saw the Spirit of God descending like
  a dove and alighting on him." (Matthew 3:16, NRSV)

🙌 Heavenly Dove,[28]
  as You drew your Holy Child,
  full of beauty,
  from the waters of baptism,
  You gave birth to the possibility
      of new life for all humanity.
  Draw us into the circle of your celestial wings:
  that, safe in the tenderness of your care,
  we grow, like Christ, in wisdom and favor
      with You;
  for You, Star of Venus,
  ascended Sophia's Breath
  to deliver your people from the jaws of death,[29]
  Blessed Trinity now and forever! Amen.

LAMENT ON THE FORCIBLE BAPTISM OF FOREIGNERS

🙌 Dovewoman,
  in the Jesus movement You opened your arms
      to the lost and forsaken ones
  and gave dignity and purpose to those who had
      been exploited by others.
  You came in simplicity to the brokenhearted,
  and gave hope and courage to your people.

How then could You permit the conquest of nations
        in the name of Christ,
allowing your missionaries to exert power over others
through enslavement dressed in Christian language?
Violence was justified through missionary zeal.
We took away the self-esteem of peoples
        who knew You in their own ways,
wiped out their languages and traditions,
considered them lower than humankind
and treated them like animals; abuse was rampant.
We did not seek to understand who they were
        or what they cared about.
Our minds were dense with the expectations
        we superimposed on them;
thickheaded, we could not see their beauty
        nor discern your face in theirs.
We imaged them to be full of evil and mischievous
        intent.
We provoked them to acts of desperation:
those who refused to submit died by sword
        or by fire or cast themselves from high ledges
        onto boulders far below.
The river rushes even yet over the memory
        of their bones.[30]
Where was your motherly compassion,
        longing to gather your children into safety?
Why did You not strike your church with plagues
        as You did to the Egyptians long ago?
Must we carry the burden of this sin forever?
It is too heavy for us!

Yet, even now You come to us in love
and lift the weight of transgression from the backs
        of your people.
The gentleness of your touch causes us to weep
        with remorse;

the clarity of your gaze appeals to us to take responsibility
    for our deeds.
You call us to make reparation to those
    our forebears have victimized.

Gracious Spirit, we cling to You;
do not leave us to the consequences of the deeds of
    our ancestors.
Open our hearts to care for others as surely as You
    tend our needs.
For You are WomanChrist,[31] our All-in-All;
You sustain people everywhere and give us hope.
Amen.

Epiphany 2

ONE WHO CARRIES US IN THE WOMB OF CREATION

- "And now Yahweh has spoken, who formed me in the womb
  to be his servant, . . . to re-unite Israel to him. . . .'I shall make
  you a light to the nations so that my salvation may reach the
  remotest parts of earth.'" (Isaiah 49:5–6, NJB)

  ☙ One Who Carries Us
  in the Womb of Creation,
  You have brought us into the world
  to make us partners in drawing all things
      into unity with You.
  Cherish us with your gentle nearness:
  that, filled with the vitality of your love,
  our lives become signs to the nations
      of your saving powers.
  Womb of All,[32]
  Nestling Child,
  You are the Spirit Who Empowers Us.
  Amen.

Epiphany 3

OLD FISHERWOMAN

- "And [Jesus] said to them, 'Follow me, and I will make you fish for people.'" (Matthew 4:19, NRSV)

     ✤ Old Fisherwoman,
    You cast your net of love
    into the sea of humanity,
    and gently draw us to Yourself.
    Make us the food
    of your Eucharistic presence:
    that, given to those in need,
    we become your sustaining power
        in the world;
    Woman of the Sea,
    Divine Child,
    You are the Source of Life and Joy.
    Amen.

Epiphany 4

FUNNYWOMAN

- "Consider your own call, brothers and sisters: not many of you were wise by human standards. . . . But God chose what is foolish in the world to shame the wise. . . . He is the source of your life in Christ Jesus, who became for us wisdom from God." (1 Corinthians 1:26–27, 30, NRSV)

     ✤ Funnywoman,
    in outrageous costume and painted face
    You turn cartwheels across heaven and earth,
    and upset the patterns of human expectation.
    Make us comediennes for Christ's sake:

> that, playing out the drama of your redemption,
> we become agents of your transformation
>   of the world.
> Mother-Trickster,
> Foolish Wisdom,
> You are the Spirit Who Teases Us into Truth! Amen.

Epiphany 5

DANCE OF MYSTERY

- "I came to you . . . not . . . with any brilliance of oratory...to
  announce to you the mystery of God . . . [but] only . . . knowledge of Jesus, and of him as the crucified Christ." (1
  Corinthians 2:1–2, NJB)

> Dance of Mystery,
>   as You swirl past us
>   in the ballroom of this earth,
>   the flowing of your gown scatters wisdom
>   in its wake,
>   and powers and principalities shift.
> Brush near us with the touch
>   of your Divine Love:
> that, drawn into the rhythm
>   of your circling,
> we step with joy into your plan
>   of redemption for the Universe.
> Ebb and Tide,
> You are the One Who Flows Forever.
> Amen.

Epiphany 6

To Ursula

MOTHER BEAR[33]

- "You have heard that it was said to those of ancient times, 'You shall not murder.' . . . But I say . . . that if you are angry with a brother or sister, you will be liable to judgment." (Matthew 5:21-22, NRSV)

- Feminist theologians suggest that scriptures which forbid anger may be relevant to men who in patriarchal tradition have been allowed to vent their anger and may need to curb their violence. In the past, however, women have not been allowed to acknowledge their anger at those who oppress them; this anger may turn inward and become low self-esteem, depression, and even madness.[34]

> ❧ Mother Bear,
> out of the fierceness of your love for us
> You watch over us night and day,
> ready to stand between us and any
>   who would do us harm.
> Be the fire within who nurtures us:
> that, energized by the ardor
>   of your protection,
> we use our anger to bring about justice
> for people who are oppressed and stricken.
> Strength in Time of Need,
> Dance of Anger,[35]
> You are the Courage of the Vulnerable Ones.
> Amen.

Epiphany 7

DIVINE BEGGARWOMAN

- "Give to everyone who begs from you, and do not refuse anyone who wants to borrow from you." (Matthew 5:42, NRSV)

🙠 Divine Beggarwoman,
   You poke through the garbage
      of the human spirit,
   in quest of the hidden treasure
      of our souls.
   Open our eyes to your presence
   in the lost and neglected ones
      of the world:
   that, turning aside from our
      prejudices,
   we minister to them in your Name.
   Mother of All,
   Outcast One,
   You are the Spirit Who Brings Us Home.
   Amen.

Epiphany 8

BREAST-FEEDING MOTHER

- "Can a woman forget her baby at the breast, feel no pity for
  the child she has borne? Even if these were to forget, I shall
  not forget you. Look, I have engraved you on the palms of my
  hands, your ramparts are ever before me." (Isaiah 49:15, NJB)

- "To hunger for her is to feed and to taste. . . ."—Hadewijch of
  Brabant[36]

🙠 Breast-Feeding Mother,
   the milk of your kindness
   and your look of love sustain us

long after we are weaned.
Awaken us to the recognition
that your commitment to us is forever:
that, nourished by your constancy,
we grow in strength and generosity.
Source of Life,
Bread of Heaven,
You are the Wine That Bubbles and Overflows!
Amen.

Transfiguration of Our Lord

SHEKINAH[37]

- "Cloud covered the mountain. The glory of Yahweh rested on Mount Sinai and the cloud covered it for six days. On the seventh day Yahweh called to Moses from inside the cloud. . . . Moses went right into the cloud and went on up the mountain." (Exodus 24:15–16, 18, NJB)

- "[Peter] was still speaking when suddenly a bright cloud covered them with shadow, and suddenly from the cloud there came a voice which said, 'This is my Son, the Beloved; he enjoys my favor. Listen to him.'" (Matthew 17:5, NJB)

 ❧ Glory of Yahweh,
     invisible yet known and felt,
     You cover us with the mists of time,
     and draw us close beneath the canopy
          of your sacred space.
     Open our hearts and minds
          to knowledge of You:
     that, luminous with the power of your love,
     we embody your goodness to all the earth.
     Ancient Mother,
     Beloved Companion,
     You are the Fire of Eternity. Amen.

The Season of Lent

— ❧ —

LENT IS OUR "ENCHANTED FOREST" where we are lured by Sophia to "places we would rather not go."[38] In Lent we begin the difficult process of breaking free from our childlike notions of the Mother, of ourselves, of others, and of life itself. We focus on that which is not attractive about ourselves, our failures, and the limits of our gifts and possibilities. We begin to make a realistic assessment of who we truly are and who it is we might become. We ache with longing and need. We rebel and do reckless things. We are afraid of the future. Eros comes to us in the chaos of sexual desire amidst the confusion of what to do with our whirling feelings. We hang back from connection with others; we plunge in; we retreat.

We are alive with a kind of vital expectation of we know not what; yet there is a stirring within us, a longing for some unknown union that we can only imperfectly imagine. The Divine becomes for us a Promise of future joy, Sophia's Song that draws us further into the mystery of life. She is the Woman of the Moon who infuses us with a sense of our sexuality. She is the Stream of Our Desire and the Spiritwoman who touches us with her earthy hand and breathes vitality and hope into us. She is Wisdom being born.

General Prayers

PROMISE OF SPRING

   ❧ Promise of Spring,
     in the midst of dark winter,
     You awaken us to hope
     and the expectation of warmth
       and new life.
     Stir within us a longing
       to be one with You:
     that, pushing our roots deep
       into your earthiness,
     we stretch forward to claim the joy
       of your resurrection in creation;
     Giver of the Vision of Shalom,
     Delicate Blossom,
     You are the Messenger of Good News.
     Amen.

ENCHANTED FOREST[39]

- "She will give . . . the bread of understanding to eat, and the water of wisdom to drink." (Ecclesiasticus 15:3, JB)

- "As we grow older, Sophia takes us inside to places where we would rather not go. She urges us to let go of old, worn-out beliefs that stifle our growth."[40]

   ❧ Enchanted Forest,
     You are the Mystery into whom we are drawn
     along paths scented with moss and evergreen.
     Protect us as we search for You amidst the brambles,
       the blood-red berries,
     the multiple hands of devil's claws snatching at
       our hair,
       our clothes, and our souls:

that, discovering You in the midst of darkness,
we flourish with You in the light of your Love.
Grove of the Dance of Wisdom,
Woodland of Our Desire,
You are our Primeval Friend forever and ever.
Amen.

Ash Wednesday

MOTHER BATHING A CHILD

- "Have mercy on me, O God, according to your steadfast love.
  . . . Wash me thoroughly from my iniquity, and cleanse me
  from my sin." (Psalm 51:1–2, NRSV)

๑ Womangod,
  as a mother plunges her child
    into sudsy water
  and scrubs away the dirt and sweat
    of the day's activities,
  You cleanse us from all that would harm us
    and others.
  Invite us to come to You with open hearts:
  that, restored to our original innocence,
  we stand before You with confidence
    and joy.
  One Who Sees All Things,
  Lover of Our Souls,
  You are the Flow of Warmth
  that heals the earth. Amen.

Lent 1

To Maureen

SONG OF SOPHIA

- "Then Jesus was led up by the Spirit into the wilderness to be tempted by the devil." (Matthew 4:1, NRSV)

🙟 Song of Sophia,
  You draw us into the wilderness
      of our own hearts
  in quest of your truth.
  Enthrall us with your serenade of love:
  that, turning from shame and self-deception,
  we become lovers of all the world
  and join the chorus of your hymn
  that soothes and heals this planet.
  Music of the Spheres,
  One Who Touches Our Innermost Being,
  You are the Lyric of Love's Song Unknown.[41]
  Amen.

Lent 2

WOMAN OF THE CRESCENT MOON

- "Now there was a Pharisee named Nicodemus, a leader of the Jews. He came to Jesus by night and said to him, 'Rabbi, we know that you are a teacher who has come from God; for no one can do these signs that you do apart from the presence of God.' Jesus answered him, 'Very truly, I tell you, no one can see the kingdom of God without being born from above.'" (John 3:1–3, NRSV)

🙟 Woman of the Crescent Moon,
  You brighten the night sky with soft splendor,
  and touch the earth with your fertile power.[42]
  Draw all that is in heaven and earth

into the orbit of your gentle spiral:
that, infused with the light of your love,
we enter into the fullness of your Glory;
for You are our Vision of Truth,
Sophia's Child,
the Luminous Energy of the Universe. Amen.

Note: for prayer related to John 4:1–42 (Lutheran lectionary), see LIVING WATER, Lent 3. For prayer related to Genesis 12:1–8, see MOTHER OF SARAH AND ALL HUMANITY, Lent 2, vol. B of *Seasons of the Feminine Divine* (1993).

Lent 3

LIVING WATER

- "The woman said to [Jesus], 'Sir, give me this water, so that I may never be thirsty.'" (John 4:15, NRSV)

☙ Living Water,
    You well up from the center
        of the Universe
    to nourish your creation.
    As the woman of Samaria drew water
        for Jesus, a stranger,
    give of Yourself to quench
    the thirsting of our souls:
    that, satisfied by the nectar
        of your love,
    we reach out in compassion
    to all who hunger for You.
    Stream of Our Desire,
    Pool of Wisdom,
    You flow through Time
    like a mighty River,
    Womangod forever and ever.
        Amen.

Lent 4

SPIRITWOMAN

- "Then Samuel took the horn of oil, and anointed [David] in the presence of his brothers; and the spirit of the Lord came mightily upon David from that day forward." (1 Samuel 16:13, NRSV)

- "The neighbors and those who had seen [the blind man] before as a beggar began to ask, 'Is this not the man who used to sit and beg?' . . . He kept saying, 'I am the man. . . . The man called Jesus made mud, spread it on my eyes, and said to me, 'Go to Siloam and wash.' Then I went and washed and received my sight.'" (John 9:8–11, NRSV)

℘ Spiritwoman,
    at your earthy touch we are reborn to wholeness
        with You and one another.
Keep us from blindness of heart,
and endow us with the fire of your compassion:
that, freed from the need to defend ourselves,
we welcome all who nurture your creation;
Heavenly Dove,
with the kiss of your devotion
You heal every nook and cranny of the Universe.
Amen.

Lent 5

GODDESS OF MARTHA[43]

- "I will put my spirit within you, and you shall live." (Ezekiel 37:14, NRSV)

- "Martha said to Jesus, 'Lord, if you had been here, my brother would not have died. But even now I know that God will give you whatever you ask of him.' Jesus said to her, 'Your brother will rise again.' Martha said to him, 'I know that he will rise again in the resurrection on the last day.' Jesus said to her, 'I am the resurrection and the life. Those who believe in me...will live, and everyone who lives and believes in me will never die. Do you believe this?' She said to him, 'Yes, Lord, I believe that you are the Messiah, the Son of God, the one coming into the world.'" (John 11:21–17, NRSV)

℘ Sister Who Dwells in the Shadows,
  through Christ You brought Lazarus
      from the grave,
  and filled with gladness the hearts
      of those who loved him.
  Give us the faith of Martha:
  that we join with her to confess
  You as the Savior of the World
  and, like her, live out our lives
  proclaiming the good news of your coming.
  Crucified and Risen One,
  Presence of New Life among Us,
  You heal with passion
      the dis-ease of this planet. Amen.

LAMENT ON THE VENERATION OF PETER AND PAUL ABOVE
OTHER DISCIPLES

℘ Grandmother of Our Ancestors,
  in ancient times You lighted the paths of the matriarchs
  and shone forth in their hearts and actions.
  Nevertheless, there came a day when You turned
      your face from women
  although they were created in the beauty of your image.
  You allowed the intelligent and powerful to be
      pushed aside, their Wisdom overturned:
  everything they had learned of You was reversed and
      repudiated.
  The new religion was enforced at the point of death;

your chosen people ravaged the lands and bodies and
hearts of the matriarchs and their daughters.

Yet when the hour was right, You sent us Jesus,
bronzed by the sun, his body wiry and nimble as a sheep;
impudent but able to charm, full of goodwill but single-
minded in purpose.
Born of a woman, He knew the pain of poverty and
oppression.
Your beloved Child sought out the marginalized and
exploited ones.
He straightened the back of the bent-over woman,
and revived the daughter of Jairus.
He restored health to the woman with a hemorrhage
and brought sanity to the bruised psyche
of Mary Magdalene.[44]
Women followed Jesus in droves and became his disciples.
Your Spirit of Wisdom once more flowed through
their bodies and minds.
They preached and baptized;
they presided over the Eucharist and gave leadership
in the early church.

Why then, did You permit their memory to be obscured?
The stories of their work to be lost?
The records of their teachings destroyed?
The apostolic succession of their gentle touch forgotten
and left behind?
How could You allow your Church to become a fiefdom
of men who exerted power over others,
a club "for males only" in which women were seen
as inferior and lacking?
In the power struggles of the early church, why did
You permit the names of Peter and Paul
to dominate our tradition,
their gifts and their weaknesses giving masculine
shape to our community?

How we long for a woman's view!
How we mourn the loss of her ministrations!

Open the door to the women of our tradition!
Bring back the stories that have been lost to us!
Give us once more our connection to our beginnings;
allow us to feel the touch of the hand of Mary
    Magdalene, Apostle of the Apostles.
Give her her rightful place in our tradition,
    beside Sarah and Miriam, Esther and Ruth.
Restore Martha and Mary of Bethany, Joanna and
    Mary the mother of Jesus.
Return to us Priscilla, Lydia, Phoebe and the other
    women missionaries and leaders of house churches.

Open wide the hearts of your people, Mother of Creation!
For You are the Tree of the Knowledge of Good and Evil,
Wisdom emerging from the ancient past to flow in our
    present,
carrying us into your future to live with You in love
    forever. Amen.

Prayers for Holy Week

IN HOLY WEEK, "LEAF BY LEAF BY LEAF," we examine and embrace our deep woundedness.[45] We struggle in the throes of the death of our old self. We resist. We do not want to let go of what we are or who we have been. We want to enter into New Being, but as who we are. We do not want to change, not even the worst of our bad habits or distorted attitudes. The more we resist, the more we choke out our life, and the farther we find ourselves from new life. As Mother Pelican the Divine chooses to die in and with us, to nurture us even in the midst of death. As She anointed Christ, so Goddess anoints us for our burial. She refuses to punish us for our stubbornness; She will never strike us; rather She continues with us as the Shekinah accompanied her people into exile, into the consequences of our human error and limitation. She washes our dead bodies and contains us once more in the darkness of her womb. Like the women who followed dead Jesus to the tomb, She wails and tears her clothes. She will not depart from us even in death. She buries herself with us in the tomb of our despair.

We come to know who we are, what the reality of our situation is, for what we will live—and die. We touch earth and begin to put down roots. As chaos fades, eros leads us into relationships with greater commitment. Knowing and loving ourselves and knowing we are loved by Goddess, we become ready to let go of fear, to love others, and to give ourselves in trust.

Passion Sunday

MOTHER PELICAN

- A medieval tradition depicts Christ as a mother pelican who was understood to pierce her own breast so that her children could survive by feeding from her blood.[46]

- Simeon prophesied that a sword would pierce the heart of Mary, the Mother of Jesus (Luke 2:34–5). The image of Mary standing at the foot of the cross weeping gives us a picture of the grief of the Divine at the suffering of Jesus. A parallel exists as well between the blood from the mother's heart and the blood from Jesus' side.

    ❧ Mother Pelican,
    You pierce your own heart
    so that your children may live.
    Fill us with your steadfast love:
    that, dying with You,
    we also rise with You to dwell forever
    in the Land that flows with milk and honey.
    Bird of Paradise,
    Crucified One,
    You are the Spirit who flies to the ends of the earth.
    Amen.

HONORIA'S LAMENT

- In the biblical record Pilate's wife has no name. "Honoria" means "honorable."[47]

    ❧ Mistress of Creation,
    in my helplessness I cry out to You!
    For all of my power and influence I am worth nothing,
    shrugged aside and dismissed.
    My words are taken lightly;

to men who rule I am no one —
a decoration, a symbol of prestige,
a bed partner, the mother of sons and no daughters!
How is it that You have made me to be impotent
even when I have the ear of the Governor?
Why is it that I feel strong in myself,
        but my efforts are in vain?
There is a person — a simple down-to-earth man —
        who speaks wisely, who is gentle —
why he takes children into his arms to bless them!
My servant women told me about this Jesus,
how he opens a new way to be in relationship with You.

Queen of Earth and Heaven,
Jesus cares for the poor and the hungry,
        the lost and broken ones.
Blessed Mother, the very image of his loving face
        is imprinted on my soul.
When You called to me in the night, warning me that this
        gentle man was to come to harm,
I awoke trembling and weeping; I could no longer sleep
but paced the ramparts of our great house until dawn.
When the old woman, the one who is blind in one eye,
brought my breakfast, I learned that Jesus was here,
        in our own palace,
a prisoner charged with treason!
Yet I know that he is neither traitor nor a blasphemer
        of your Name!
Hurrying my ladies-in-waiting with my morning grooming,
I hastened to my desk to write a letter to my husband.
I appealed to him from the depths of my heart
        to resist the pressures of the Herodians.
I told him of my dream and how it was that he held the fate
        of the Universe between his own fingers.
I prayed for your power to go with this letter and implored
        your mercy for your holy Child!

Pilate knows me; he knows that I have had portents and
   intuitions before.
Yet I am told by one close to him that he regarded my
   letter as frivolous, as the outpour of lesser female
   emotions;
he saw my words as flights of fancy, as fiction
   unworthy of serious attention.
He washed his hands of me.

Fire of Justice, cleanse this earth of bigotry and prejudice!
Enflame the hearts of humankind with the passion
   of your love for all people,
that we be healed by your Divine Radiance in which
   we will bask forever with Jesus, our Beloved,
in the warmth of your covering Spirit. Amen.

Monday in Holy Week

PASSIONATE GODDESS

* "A woman came to [Jesus] with an alabaster jar of very costly
  ointment, and she poured it on his head as he sat at the table."
  (Matthew 26:7, NRSV)

  Passionate Goddess,
     while Jesus' disciples fell into confusion
        and poised for flight,
     You comforted him through the gentleness
        of a woman's hands
     as she anointed his head with costly oil.[48]
  Make us bold like her:
     that, entering into the pain of others,
     we consecrate our lives to the salvation
        of the world.
  Goddess of Life, Death and Resurrection,
  You heal us with your Glory, world without end.
  Amen.

Tuesday in Holy Week

FOOLISH WISDOM

> ❧ Foolish Wisdom,
>   You turn upside down our way of thinking,
>   and astonish us with the mystery of your love.
>   Teach us to be your clowns for justice:
>   that, playing out the gospel wherever we are,
>   we become agents of your transformation
>   of the world;
>   Mother-Trickster,
>   Crucified and Risen One,
>   You are the Spirit Who Teases Us into Truth. Amen.

Wednesday in Holy Week

ONE STRUCK DOWN

- "But I say to you . . . Love your enemies, do good to those who
  hate you. . . . Pray for those who abuse you. . . . Do to others
  as you would have them do to you." (Luke 6:27–31, NRSV)

- "I have offered my back to those who struck me, my cheeks to
  those who plucked my beard; I have not turned my face away
  from insult and spitting. Lord Yahweh comes to my help, this
  is why this insult has not touched me, this is why I . . . know
  that I shall not be put to shame. He who grants me saving justice is here!" (Isaiah 50:5a–8a, NJB)

> ❧ One Struck Down,
>   You did not strike back,
>   but overcame hatred with love.[49]
>   Give us the strength
>   to sustain the evil that we suffer:
>   that, empowered by our anger,

we clear our hearts and minds of fear
and work for justice and peace for all persons.
Grief-Stricken Mother,
Crucified One,
You are the Promise of New Life. Amen.

Note: See also, BATTERED WOMAN, Volume C, 82; and ONE
WHO PROWLS THE JUNGLE OF LIFE: A LAMENT FOR ONES
ABUSED, Volume C, 83.

Maundy Thursday

CLEANSING WATER

- "Then he poured water into a basin and began to wash the disciples' feet." (John 13:5, NRSV)

  ❧ Cleansing Water,
    You touch the feet of the powerful
        with your transforming love,
    and wash greed and ambition from the face
        of the earth.
    Bathe us in the coolness of yourself:
    that, healed of human division,
    we are restored to the Land of your Shalom.
    Ocean of Our Desire,
    Pool of Wisdom,
    You are the Rainstorm who transforms
        the wasteland into a field of flowers. Amen.

GODDESS PRESENT IN THE ACTION OF THE WASHING OF FEET

- "Mary [of Bethany] took a pound of costly perfume made of
  pure nard, anointed Jesus' feet, and wiped them with her hair.
  The house was filled with the fragrance of the perfume."
  (John 12:1–8 RSV)

❧ Mother and Sister of All,
   when Mary washed the feet of Jesus
   and wiped them with her hair,
   You revealed to him the image of humility
   that he was to enact for all generations
        at the Last Supper.
   Teach us how to serve one another out of love:
   that, letting go of the slavishness of our pasts,
   we claim the freedom and dignity given us in Christ.
   Source of Wisdom,
   Anointed One,
   You are the Spirit who brings the world
        into wholeness. Amen.

Good Friday

Grieving Woman

- "A great number of the people followed [Jesus], and among
  them were women who were beating their breasts and wailing
  for him. But Jesus turned to them and said, 'Daughters of
  Jerusalem, do not weep for me, but weep for yourselves and
  your children. For the days are surely coming when they will
  say, 'Blessed are the barren, and the wombs that never bore,
  and the breasts that never nursed.'" (Luke 23:27–9 NRSV)

❧ Grieving Woman,
   we hear your anguish in the wailing
        of the women
   who followed Jesus to the cross
   and remained with Him until he died.
   Help us to know the pain You suffer
   in behalf of your people:
   that, embodying your presence,
   we comfort all who are in sorrow
   wherever we find them;
   Mother, Child and Holy Spirit,
   One Goddess forever. Amen.

Saturday in Holy Week

ROOT OF ALL LIFE

- "Like a sapling he grew up before him, like a root in arid ground." (Isaiah 53:2 NRSV)

- "Understanding is the root. The resounding Word blossoms forth from it." (Hildegard of Bingen[50])

Root of All Life,
together with your sapling Child,
You burrow in arid ground.
Anchor us in the soil of your compassion:
that from unpromising beginnings
your Word shall blossom anew
to proclaim the holiness of your creation.
Sacred Tree,
Flower of Passion,
You are the Wind that warms the earth
and brings us to new life,
Goddess Three-in-One. Amen.

The Season of Easter

AT EASTERTIDE WE WAKE UP FROM DEATH and discover ourselves in the transition of new birth. We shed our old skins, burst open the protective chrysalis, and emerge pale and fresh in the earliest form of our true selves. As we dry in the warmth of new light, we draw together the memories of times when Sophia has blessed us in our lives through the love and care of family and friends, the beauty of nature, the goodness of work, our resilience in the midst of struggle, and in the transformation of our hearts by the warmth of her numinous Presence in prayer.[51]

Recognizing ourselves as in her image, we allow the memories of her goodness to strengthen us to continue the journey. These memories remind us of our destination and of how it is that we are called to wholeness. We experience a blossoming in our hearts, a euphoria that enables us to push free from the past, and to leave resistance and death behind. Wholeheartedly, we enter into the future. Now conscious, we know we are making this pilgrimage. We strategize and make plans. The Star that once was outside of us is now within. We follow the voice of Sophia–Jesus. Eros explodes within us in our need to find completion—in our need to be in union with her.

The Divine as Midwife assists us into this new dimension of being; in her hands we experience the healing for which we have longed. She is our Song of Love; we dance; we celebrate the coming of Shalom, of Peace. We turn from our self-absorption to the suffering of the world. We prepare to become messengers of love and peace. Goddess fills us with strength and courage.

General

MORNING-GLORY

> ❧ Morning-Glory,
> You absorb the nutrients of earth's bounty
> and push your way from dark soil to the warmth
>   of light.
> You climb, You blossom forth in sapphire beauty;
> You dance and play in the wind,
> your fragile blooms swaying in serpentine
>   ecstasy.
> Flower within us this Eastertide:
> that, opening to new life,
> we leave death behind forever.
> Tender of the Gardens of Our Souls,
> Ephemeral One,
> You are the Perennial who brings us
>   into life eternal. Amen.

HOLY MIDWIFE

> • "By his great mercy he has given us a new birth into a living
>   hope through the resurrection of Jesus Christ from the dead."
>   (1 Peter 1:3, NRSV.)

> ❧ Holy Midwife,
> You transport us into the joy
> from which men give birth to infant love
> and women claim the justice of new life.
> Catch us up in the mystery of your healing
>   power:
> that, turning from our destructive ways,
> we join with You to restore this planet
>   to wholeness and hope.

Wise Healer,
Wounded Earth,
You deliver us into the garden of New Creation,
world without end. Amen.

SONG OF LOVE

- "Yahweh is my strength and my song, he has been my savior."
  (Psalm 118:14, NJB)

  ❧ Song of Love,
  You woo us with your melody of joy
  and draw us to You with the sound
      of your sweetness.
  Strengthen us with the knowledge
  that your compassion never dies:
  that, assured of a home with You for all time,
  we celebrate this Easter season.
  Holy One, we raise our voices to praise You
      forever: Alleluia! Alleluia!
  Amen.

The Easter Vigil

- The Creation Story—see the prayers for Christmas–General
  or Christmas 2.
- The Story of Salvation History—The period of judges—see the
  prayer for Advent 1 which relates to Deborah, WOMANJUDGE.
- The role of the SHEKINAH in whose shadow this story
  unfolds—see the prayers for Epiphany–General, SHEKINAH,
  or Transfiguration, SHEKINAH.
- For reference to Israel's sojourn in the wilderness, see the
  prayer for Lent 2, SONG OF SOPHIA.
- Prophetic tradition—Advent 1, WOMANJUDGE (Deborah).
- Wisdom tradition—Feast of Epiphany, WISDOM OF THE
  UNIVERSE; Lent–General, ENCHANTED FOREST; Tuesday in

Holy Week, FOOLISH WISDOM; Twenty-First Sunday of Ordinary Time, MOTHER OF WISDOM.

- The role of Mary the Mother of Jesus—see the prayer for Christmas Eve, DIVINE MOTHER.
- Reference to Jesus' baptism—see the prayer for the First Sunday after Epiphany, HEAVENLY DOVE.
- References to Jesus' ministry—see the prayers for Lent 3, LIVING WATER, Fifth Sunday after Epiphany, DANCE OF MYSTERY.
- Jesus' suffering—see the prayer for Wednesday in Holy Week, ONE STRUCK DOWN.
- Christ today—See the prayer for the Seventh Sunday after Epiphany, DIVINE BEGGARWOMAN.
- Also see the sections on Easter Vigil in Volumes B & C of *Seasons of the Feminine Divine.*

Easter 1

SHAKER OF THIS EARTH

- "And suddenly there was a violent earthquake, for an angel of the Lord, descending from heaven came and rolled away the stone and sat on it. . . . The guards were so shaken by fear of him that they were like dead men. But the angel spoke . . . to the women, 'There is no need to be afraid. I know you are looking for Jesus. . . . He is not here, for he has risen.'" (Matthew 28:2, 4–5, NJB)

  ℘ Shaker of this Earth,
  in raising Jesus from the dead
  You unsettled powers and principalities
  and turned the stream of your Wisdom
       toward new vistas.
  Empower us your church to become
       the wave of your justice:
  that, gathering together as your Easter people,
  we celebrate with joy the coming of Shalom.

Mother Earthquake,
Christ Our Epicenter,
You transform this planet with Love. Amen.

WOMAN OF RHYTHM

- "I have loved you with an everlasting love . . . , Virgin of Israel!
  Once more in your best attire, and with your tambourines, you
  will go out dancing gaily. . . . Proclaim! Praise! Shout, 'Yahweh
  has saved his people.'" (Jeremiah 31:3–4, 7b, NJB)

⧆ Woman of Rhythm,
   draped in the colors of the New Dawn,
   your hips undulate, your body sways
   to the trill of your tambourine that shivers
       through the Universe.
   Sing out with us the joy of Christ risen!
   That, gathering your sisters and brothers
       into the circle of your creativity,
   You draw us into the dance of the cosmos
       that leads to Shalom.
   Artist of Creation,
   Whirling Spirit,
   your vitality transforms the Universe,
       alleluia! Amen.

Easter 2

TENACIOUS FLOWER

- ". . . you crucified and killed [Jesus]. . . . But God raised him
  up, having freed him from death, because it was impossible for
  him to be held in its power." (Acts 2:23, NRSV)

⧆ Tenacious Flower,
   whom cruel winter cannot hold forever,
   though given up for dead and buried,

You cling to the thread of life.
Bloom within this your church:
that, rooted with You in the Mother's warm
        earth,
we discover anew the joy of your cosmic dance.
Herald Crocus,
Blossom of Mercy,
the perfume of your Love wafts on Spirit's wings.
Amen.

ALCHEMY OF SOPHIA

- ". . . so that the genuineness of your faith—being more precious than gold that, though perishable, is tested by fire—may be found to result in praise and glory and honor when Jesus Christ is revealed." (1 Peter 1:7, NRSV)

- Divine Alchemist,
    You transform the dross of our lives
    into the gold of eternal blessing.
    Test the metal of our devotion
    by the Fire of your compassion:
    that the Elixir of your love,
    embodied in us forever,
    become the flow of your ongoing creation.
    Questing Sister,
    Crucified and Risen One,
    You are Sophia's Touch. Amen.

BREATH OF RUAH

- "Jesus said to [the disciples], . . . 'Peace be with you. As the Father has sent me, so I send you.' When he had said this, he breathed on them and said to them, 'Receive the Holy Spirit. If you forgive the sins of any, they are forgiven them; if you retain the sins of any, they are retained.'" (John 20:21–23, NRSV)

❧ Breath of Ruah,
  the moist touch of your love permeates
      our hearts forever,
  and makes us new.
  Keep us aware that in all we think
      and speak and do,
  we exercise the power to offer or withhold
  the gift of your transforming grace.
  Inspiration of the Faithful,
  Flutter of Life coming into being,
  You are the Whisper who draws us into
      kinship with You forever. Amen.

Easter 3

SOPHIA, SISTER OF ALL

- "... when they heard this, they were cut to the heart and said ...
  "what should we do?" Peter said, "Repent and be baptized ... in
  the name of Jesus Christ so that your sins may be forgiven; and you
  will receive the gift of the Holy Spirit." (Acts 2:37–8, NRSV)

- "When [Jesus] was at the table with them, he took bread,
  blessed and broke it, and gave it to them. Then their eyes were
  opened, and they recognized him; and he vanished from their
  sight. They said to each other, "Were not our hearts burning
  within us while he was talking to us on the road, while he was
  opening the scriptures to us?" (Luke 24:30–32, NRSV)

❧ Sophia, Sister of All,
  You come in mystery,
  and your entrance into the locked chambers
      of our hearts
  is as intimate as a lover's kiss.[52]
  Enable us to open our souls and bodies
  to the caress of your mercy:

that, made whole by your resurrection,
we are initiated into the community of grace
and celebrate with You the joy of Shalom;
Womangod within,
Womangod without,
Womangod All-in-All. Amen.

Note: For prayer related to 1 Peter 1:17. "If you invoke as
Father the one who judges all people impartially according to
their deeds, live in reverent fear during the time of your exile"
(NRSV), see HEAVENLY DOVE, First Sunday after Epiphany, or
QUEEN OF JUSTICE, Christmas Eve.

Easter 4

ONE WHO CALLS US INTO COMMUNITY

- "All who believed were together and had all things in common; they would sell their possessions and goods and distrib-
  ute the proceeds to all, as any had need." (Acts 2:44–5, NRSV)

- Regarding the reading from 1 Peter 2:19–25, this reading could
  be used dangerously by asking women and others to endure
  ongoing injustice: "When he was abused, he did not return
  abuse . . ." (NRSV) It is important, therefore, to emphasize
  empowerment and the moving out of oppression in this prayer.

 ✎ One Who Calls Us into Community,
    You draw us out of the oppression
        of human structures
    and set us upon the threshold
        of divine possibility.
    Help us to leave behind our victim
        selves
    and to open to the joy of empowerment
        in Christ:
    that, strengthened by our friendship with You,
    we enter into wholeness as your Easter people.

Midwife at the Birth of the End Time,
One Who Leads Us from Childhood into Maturity,
You are the Soul-Sister of Our Dreams. Amen.

See also *Seasons of the Feminine Divine*, Cycle C, LAMENT
FOR ONES ABUSED, the Second Sunday of Easter, 83.

CHAMPION OF THE OPPRESSED

- "I am the door; if any one enters by me, he will be saved, and
  will go in and out and find pasture. . . . I came that they may
  have life, and have it abundantly." (John 10:9–10, RSV)

- Some years ago I saw in a film on the revolution in Nicaragua
  campaneros marching and chanting Marian slogans. The
  vividness of these people's trust that Mary was with them
  moved me deeply. I offer the image to you in this prayer.

  🌺 Champion of the Oppressed,
  You open the door of the prisons
  where we are held captive
  and send us in quest of new life.
  Reveal to us the secrets
      of your compassion:
  that, nurtured by the power
      of your resurrection,
  we seek to share your life abundant
      with all those in need.
  Heroine of Our Dreams,
  One Who Died for Us,
  You are the path of our hope and salvation.
  Amen.

Easter 5

WINGED SHEKINAH

- "But filled with the Holy Spirit, [Stephen] gazed into heaven and saw the glory of God. . . . "Lord Jesus, receive my spirit." (Acts 7:55, 59, NRSV)

- "Like newborn infants, long for the pure, spiritual milk, so that by it you may grow into salvation—if indeed you have tasted that the Lord is good." (1 Peter 2:2, NRSV)

☙ Winged Shekinah,
  You shone in the radiance of Stephen's face
  as he gazed into the warmth of your eyes
  and received your kiss of welcome.[53]
  Give us the passion of Stephen:
  that, loving You above all else,
  we proclaim with faith your Gospel to the world.
  Numinous Presence,
  Crucified and Risen One,
  You are the Glory who transforms this earth.
  Amen.

Easter 6

OCEAN OF WISDOM

- "The God who made the world and everything in it . . . made all nations to inhabit the whole earth . . . so that they would search for God . . . and find him—though indeed he is not far from each one of us. For in him we live and move and have our being." (Acts 17:24, 26–8, NRSV)

☙ Ocean of Wisdom,
  You conceived us in Glory
  and, by the genius of your creative power,
  have brought us into Being.

Contain us within the space of infant Earth:
that, safe within your embryonic waters,
we and all creation are born whole
    into the joy of Shalom.
Womb of All,
You are the Channel of Our Desire,
the Sea that covers the earth and makes it new.
Amen.

Ascension of the Lord

BREATH OF THE PLANET EARTH

- "You will be my witnesses . . . to the ends of the earth." (Acts 1:8, NRSV)

🙟 Breath of Planet Earth,
from the flow of your energy
    all life evolves
and grows and dies and lives again.
Give us the wisdom to know the trees of the hills,
the running waters, the animals and the air itself
    as our brothers and sisters:
that, saved from exaggerating our own importance,
we live in humility, accepting the vulnerability
    and potential that is common to all nature.
Seeker of the Harmony of the Spheres,
You bring all things into one with You,
through Jesus Sophia, WomanChrist[54] forever.
Amen.

PROMISE OF SOPHIA

- "This," [Jesus] said, "is what you have heard from me; for John baptized with water, but you will be baptized with the Holy Spirit not many days from now." (Acts 1:4–5, NRSV)

- "Then [Jesus] led them out as far as Bethany, and, lifting up his hands, he blessed them. While he was blessing them, he withdrew from them and was carried up into heaven." (Luke 24:50, NRSV)

❧ Promise of Sophia,
    You come to us in gentle utterance
        and quiet discernment,
    and hearten us with the mystery
        of your presence within us.
    Open us to the anticipation
        of your ceaseless love:
    that, awakened more and more
        to your nearness,
    we are filled with the amazement
        of joy in You.
    Vow of Fidelity,
    You are the Guarantor of Life Eternal,
    Alleluia! Amen.

Easter 7

TAMER OF THE ROARING LION

- "But rejoice insofar as you are sharing Christ's sufferings, so that you may also be glad and shout for joy when his glory is revealed." (1 Peter 4:13, NRSV)

- "Discipline yourselves, keep alert. Like a roaring lion your adversary the devil prowls around, looking for someone to devour. . . . And after you have suffered for a little while, the God of all grace, who has called you to his eternal glory in Christ, will . . . restore . . . you." (1 Peter 5:8, NRSV)

❧ Tamer of the Roaring Lion,
    You banish those who would devour
        and destroy creation

and bring all things into unity with You.
Instill in us a spirit of vigilance:
that, aware of the power of evil,
we be filled with your power for good;
for You are Sophia, wise as a serpent,
the Wounded One, innocent as a dove,
and the Spirit, our Beloved,
who makes the Universe whole. Amen.

LAMENTATION ON THE BIRTH PANGS
OF THE TWENTIETH CENTURY

٪ Mother of All,
You cast us from your womb,
and we are no longer encircled in safety!
In every part of the world, structures crumble and
    fall apart and we are left without support or hope.
Where there appeared to be peace, now there is war.
Neighbor turns against neighbor; there is no mercy.
Day after day women are raped,
and starving children slaughtered in the streets.

Gracious One, we heap our confessions into your lap,
we pile them up until we can no longer see your
face—how we have sought after our own comfort
and turned our backs on the poor of the world,
how we have looked to our own kind
and refused to learn to live with those different
    from ourselves,
how we have built empires on the backs of those
    we have exploited,
and given less value to those of other races or classes
    or religions.
We refuse to listen to them or to open our hearts.
We are quick to judge, and to assert our own position.

Caught up in our addiction to material things,
we have turned away from your voice;
we do not hear the whisper of truth from your Spirit.

Must we come to total destruction before we remember
You?
Must the just desserts of our actions fall upon us,
must we lose our wealth, our friendships, and our
confidence in your providence
before we turn once more to You?
Will You bring the world to its knees in catastrophe
before we take You seriously,
before we understand that You are not only the
Comforter
but the One who prods us from our complacency?

The Devourer already crouches over us.
She swings her great tail with its claw at the end;
cities and the peoples of the cities are crushed.
She makes a show of her powers of destruction
for all the world to see.
By trickery and deceit she magnifies the strength
of her venom,
and fire rushes from her belly to melt any who stand
in her way.
No one dares to take her on.
Fear grips the heart of the nations;
there is wailing and lament in every direction.

Wise Spirit, come to us! Enter our hearts and souls and
minds with your courage and your steadfast love!
Give us a vision of the new world into which You,
with pain, bring us to birth.
Restore our faith in the mystery of your power
which is not like the world's power,

the might with which You opened a path in the
     midst of the sea,
and made dry land where once the River Jordan flowed.
Embrace us in the knowledge that your love
     permeates all things, even the tombs of the dead,
     and creates new and abundant life.

Sister of Our Hearts, we return once more to You,
for You make us the meadow on which shines
     the light of your justice;
where we were once wasteland, You bring us to blossom;
where we were lost, You have become our Compass.

Beloved Goddess, You dwell in us and we in You
     forever and ever, Alleluia! Amen.

The Season of Pentecost: the Feminine Divine as Mature Woman

(From Pentecost through June 12–18)

At Pentecost we find ourselves facing a window that opens onto a new country.[55] Sophia brings us to the opening and waits for us to make the choice. Knowing who we are, we find our voice and are ready to proclaim the good news of new life. Understanding what we will speak and live and die for, and certain that She is within us now and forever, we step out into the unknown, following the inner map of her Presence that leads us Home. Eros draws us into herself through community with other people with whom we share our common experience of the gifts She has given us. As we grow in love, we carry her Star[56] to others, bringing the gospel of her justice to the world.

In Pentecost Womangod becomes Creatress in a new way. She is no longer the One who gives physical birth; rather, She creates the ongoing life of the Universe. As Mother, She teaches us to mother others. As Creatress, She functions as Artist and is the source of our creativity. She is the abundance of the Love of which the mature woman is capable. She is the Energy that moves all that is. She is manifest in women wherever they are at work and in every occupation: Woman Farmer, Skilled Builder, Carpenter, Laborer, Tax Collector, Banker. We hear her cries of anguish in the supplications of the Beggarwoman and in the laments of women who are exploited in the workplace.

As Matriarch, Womangod offers us the wisdom to face reality. In her graciousness She welcomes the lost and the needy, comforts those who mourn, and gives rest to the weary. As Convenor of the Quilting Bee, She is the One who initiates creative activity in others. In her wisdom She loves all that exists: the errant child, beasts of the field, and even what humans view as weeds, plants of negative or no account. She offers her life as food for the hungry.

As Queen of earth and heaven, Womangod lives in harmony with creation. Serene, She is capable of calming storms. Unafraid of the opinions of others, She is able to ask for what She needs. She is both practical and wise. As Midwife, She enables others to give birth to new life, and She helps us to become midwives to others. She carries those who cannot yet care for themselves. She hears all who call upon her Name. She is the power within the Universe; yet there is nowhere we can go that She is not. She is benevolent Employer, Lady, and Landowner. She is the resurgence of the Divine as Great Goddess in our time.

As the One who has struggled with and within us, the Feminine Divine is also the One who brings us home. Full of compassion, She is Friend of the Homeless, Heart of the Universe, One who bears the burden of the world, and One who weeps at the plight of refugees. Gatherer of all good memories, Womangod receives our faithful devotion and helps us to discover soulmates with whom to share our journeys. As Oil of Gladness She anoints us into mission and ministry. As Lioness, She keeps us on the right path and guards and nurtures us on our pilgrimage. Finally, at the Last Day, our Shepherdess scoops us into her arms and carries us into the Land of Her Shalom to live forever in the wonder of her Love.

General Prayers

WINDOW OF OUR BEING

    ✤ Window of Our Being,
      You open us to freedom from the boxes
        of our limited perceptions.
      Draw us to the vision of your hope
        for the Universe:
      that, letting go of the clutter of our resistance
        to your love,
      we open to the wonder of your transforming
        power.
      Liberating Goddess,
      Prism of Our Courage,
      You are the Vista of New Possibility,
      world without end. Amen

WEAVER OF THE EARTH AND SKY

    ✤ Weaver of the Earth and Sky,
      You shape our lives with the running
        of your shuttle,
      back and forth, back and forth,
      amongst your threaded Glory.
      Fashion in us designs rich with your grace
        and loving kindness:
      that, knowing we are only part of the whole,
      we rejoice to become one with You
        in the tapestry of your Universe.
      Maker of New Life,
      Pattern of Our Desire,
      You are the Flow of Divine Creativity. Amen.

MOTHER WHO TUCKS US IN

> ❧ Mother of All,
>   as You draw the blanket of night about us,
>   You tuck us into the safe space of your love.
>   Be present with us in our dreaming:
>   that the anxieties of our todays and tomorrows
>   be healed by your redemptive touch,
>   and we meet the future with strength
>   born of your movement in our lives;
>   Evening Star,
>   Child of Glory,
>   You are the Whisper of Wisdom. Amen.

The Feast of Pentecost

RAINWOMAN

- "Thus says the Lord who made you, who formed you in the womb and will help you. . . . Do not fear. . . . For I will pour water on the thirsty land . . . my spirit upon your descendants, and my blessing on your offspring. They shall spring up like a green tamarisk, like willows by flowing streams." (Isaiah 44:2–4, NRSV)

- ". . . I will pour out my Spirit upon all flesh, and your sons and your daughters shall prophesy, and your young men shall see visions, and your old men shall dream dreams. Even upon my slaves, both men and women, in those days I will pour out my Spirit; and they shall prophesy." (Acts 2:17b–18, NRSV)

- "'Peace be with you.' When [Jesus] had said this, he breathed on them and said, . . . Receive the Holy Spirit.'" (John 20:21–22, NRSV)

- "[Jesus] cried out, 'let anyone who is thirsty come to me. . . . As the Scripture has said, *Out of the believer's heart [belly] shall flow rivers of living water.*'" (John 7:37–38, NRSV)

❧ Rainwoman,
  You fulfill your promise of redemption
  through the pouring out of yourself
      upon the sun-scorched land
  that thirsts, that cries out, for your
      nourishment.
  Raise up within us the flowing stream
      of your Wisdom:
  that, fed by your mercy and compassion,
  we bring into blossom your justice and peace,
      world without end. Amen.

Trinity Sunday

ENERGY THAT MOVES THE UNIVERSE

- "... remember, I am with you always, to the end of the days."
  (Matthew 28:20, NRSV)

- "Do you not realize that Jesus Christ is in you? . . . live in
  peace." (2 Corinthians 13:5, 11, NRSV)

❧ Energy that moves the Universe,
  You have created this earth from the abundance
      of your Love,
  and made it the garden of human community.
  Blaze within us as the Christ Spirit:
  that, not clinging to anything except You alone,
  we reverence You in every element of this planet.
  One of Constancy,
  One of Change,
  You are the Lover of All Creation. Amen.

Sixth Sunday in Ordinary Time (May 8–14)

To Marge

WOMAN FARMER

- "I fed you with milk, not solid food, for you were not ready.
  . . . Even now you are not ready." (1 Corinthians 3:2, NRSV)

- "I [Paul] planted, Apollos watered, but God gave the growth.
  . . . For we are God's servants, working together; you are God's
  field." (1 Corinthians 3:6–9, NRSV)

- I have great-aunts and a mother-in-law who were farmers with
  their spouses. The protagonist in the novel *Judith,* was a
  woman farming on her own.[57]

> ❧ Woman Farmer,
> You scatter the grains of your Wisdom
>   into the soil of our hearts
> and nourish us with devotion that never fails.
> Make us workers in the field of this earth:
> that, cultivating with You the seeds of peace,
> all creation be brought into the granary
>   of your Love.
> Producer and Germinator of the unity of the spheres,
> You are Goddess Three-in-One, world without end.
> Amen.

See also WOMANJUDGE, Advent 1 and Christmas Day, 30 and
39, regarding Matthew 5:17–20, NRSV, "Therefore, whoever
breaks one of the least of these commandments, and teaches
others to do the same, will be called least in the kingdom of
heaven; but whoever does them and teaches them will be
called great in the kingdom of heaven."; Ecclesiasticus (Sirach)
15:15, NRSV, "If you will, you can keep the commandments,
and to act faithfully is a matter of your own choice."; and

Deuteronomy 30:16, NRSV, "If you obey the commandments of the Lord your God, . . . by loving the Lord your God, walking in his ways, and observing his commandments, decrees, and ordinances, then you shall live."

Seventh Sunday in Ordinary Time (May 15–21)

SKILLED BUILDER

- "According to the grace of God given to me [Paul], like a skilled master builder I laid a foundation, and someone else is building on it. Each builder must choose with care how to build on it. For no one can lay any foundation other than the one that has been laid; that foundation is Jesus Christ." (1 Corinthians 3:10–11, NRSV)

- "So let no one boast about human leaders. For all things are yours, whether Paul or Apollos or Cephas or the world or life or death or the present or the future—all belong to you, and you belong to Christ, and Christ belongs to God." (1 Corinthians 3:21–23, NRSV)

  ❧ Woman Mason,
  You mix us, the clay of your earth,
     with the straw of your grace
  and bake us in the warmth of your womb.
  Position us in the building up of your church:
  that, set in the right place at the right time,
  we proclaim the good news of Christ
  to those who long to be with You.
  Woman of Wisdom,
  Woman of Skill,
  You are the Builder of Shalom. Amen.

Eighth Sunday in Ordinary Time (May 22–28)

BEGGARWOMAN

- "When you reap the harvest of your land, you shall not reap to the very edges of your field, or gather the gleanings of the harvest . . . or . . . the fallen grapes of your vineyard; you shall leave them for the poor and the alien . . . you shall not keep for yourself the wages of a laborer until morning . . . revile the deaf or put a stumbling block before the blind . . . you shall love your neighbor as yourself." (Leviticus 19:9–10, 13–14, NRSV)

- "It is the Lord who acquits me." (1 Corinthians 4:4, NRSV)

- "Give to everyone who begs from you, and do not refuse anyone who wants to borrow from you." (Matthew 5:42, NRSV)

- This image of Beggarwoman comes from Mexico where women in black take on an almost stylized posture of supplication in churches, at shrines, and along the streets of the cities.

   ❧ Beggarwoman,
      dressed in black You sit on the curbside,
      your arm held in supplication,
      your palm arched in classic gesture.
      The thinness of your hand, the gauntness of your face
      speak to the truth of your predicament.
      Save us from the malnourishment of Spirit
      that robs us of compassion:
      that, rushing to empower the poor and the hungry,
      we give all that we have and all that we are
         for your sake.
      Mother of Humanity,
      Vulnerable One,
      You are Womanspirit who calls us
         to live in You forever. Amen.

Ninth Sunday in Ordinary Time (May 29–June 4)

WISEWOMAN CARPENTER

- "Everyone who listens to these words of mine and acts on them will be like a sensible man who built his house on rock. Rain came down, floods rose, gales blew and hurled themselves against that house, and it did not fall." (Matthew 7:24–25, NJB)

❧ Wisewoman Carpenter,
You raise up the house of creation
on a foundation of stone
and secure the crossbeams with the nails
of your steadfast love.
Teach us the craft of your compassion:
that, discerning the blueprint of your salvation,
we work with You to bring your Universe
into completion.
Friend of Workers,
Common Laborer,
You are the One Who Calls Us to Wisdom. Amen.

Tenth Sunday in Ordinary Time (June 5–11)
To Carol

WOMAN PHYSICIAN

- "[Jesus] said, 'Those who are well have no need of a physician, but those who are sick. Go and learn what this means, I desire mercy, not sacrifice.'" (Matthew 9:12–13, NRSV)

❧ Woman Physician,
You long to bind up the wounds of Creation
and heal the pollution of greed and power-over[58]
that contaminates this earth.
Out of the vast store of your knowledge,

prescribe for us the medicine of your Love:
that, experiencing the tenderness of your touch,
we and this planet open to the healing of your grace.
Mother of Mercy,
Compassionate One,
You coax the Universe into health and wholeness,
    world without end. Amen.

Eleventh Sunday in Ordinary Time (June 12–18)

WOMAN LABORER

- "Then [Jesus] said to his disciples, 'The harvest is plentiful, but the laborers are few; therefore ask the Lord of the harvest to send out laborers into his harvest.'" (Matthew 9:37–38, NRSV)

❧ Woman Laborer,
    You rise before sunup
    and return home after nightfall;
    You stoop with the weight of your work;
        your spirit faints.
    Be in our day-to-day struggle to survive:
    that, strengthened by your presence with us,
    we are freed to work for justice and human dignity.
    Mother of the World,
    Woman Carpenter,
    You are the Courage of the poor and downtrodden!
    Amen.

LAMENT FOR UNJUST WORKING CONDITIONS
FOR WOMEN WORLDWIDE

❧ Queen of earth and heaven,
    where are You in the sweat shops of the East

among the poor women who slave in airless buildings;
they bake in the tropical heat as they sow lace trim
    on a woman's undergarment,
or gather folds of silk into graceful waistlines
    upon which they fasten a rose of velvet?
Where are You in the dimly lit rooms
where women squint as they assemble mini-calculators
until they lose their sight and are left helpless, homeless
    and hungry?
Where are You in the plantations of Central America
    while male supervisors prowl at leisure,
not allowing their female workers to break
    for more than a few minutes no matter how
    much their backs hurt,
seeing that women's hands never stop moving,
making sure that, if quotas are not filled on time,
someone else is hired who can meet the target?
Where are You when their children roam unsupervised
    in the streets of the uncaring city?
Where are You when the young girl, pregnant
    but with no husband,
is cast into the streets to become a prostitute or starve?
Everywhere women are exploited; everywhere they suffer.
Do You not hear their sighs of misery and resignation?

Take your hands from your ears!
Unwrap the scarves which You have wound about
    your head to muffle the sound of our cries!
Allow the heat of our anguish to scorch the innermost
    reaches of your heart,
where your steadfast mercy dwells and never fails.

For You created in us the gift of labor and the love of
    occupation.
You sent us out from the garden with the capacity
    to build community through work.

You give us abilities and the desire to become co-creators
    with You of a world that never ends.
Divine Laborer, Blessed Womangod,
make us one with You in bringing in your New Creation
where each person has dignity and life abundant,
world without end! Amen.

Prayers after Pentecost:
Womangod as Matriarch

(Sundays in Ordinary Time, June 19–August 6)

Twelfth Sunday in Ordinary Time (June 19–23)

WHISPER OF TRUTH

- "Do not be afraid of [those who killed Jesus]. There is nothing covered up that will not be uncovered, nothing hidden that will not be made known. What I say to you in the dark you must repeat in broad daylight; what you hear whispered you must shout from the housetops. Do not fear those who kill the body. . . . Fear . . . rather [the one] who is able to destroy both soul and body." (Matthew 10:26–28, NRSV)

- Ana Maria Rodas writes of her feelings about her aunt who was murdered during the war in Guatamala: "I inhabit a cemetery. I have been making myself old here beside my dead ones. I don't need friends. To love frightens me because I have loved many and lost them all in the war. My pain is enough for me. It helps me to live these bleak sunrises, this awakening blankness, these lonely nights, this incessant loss."[59]

   Whisper of Truth,
     You share with us the mystery of your Love
     and open our eyes to the reality of the human
       condition.

Give us the courage to be the voice of your
      compassion:
that, turning aside from the rationalizations
      of our defenses,
we find the strength to speak in behalf of
      the poor and the oppressed.
Grandmother who gathers her children
      to her bosom,
Peasant Woman, murdered and thrown into a
      mass grave,
You are Spiritwoman who nudges the conscience
      of the wealthy and powerful. Amen.

Thirteenth Sunday in Ordinary Time (June 26–July 2)

WELCOMER OF THE LOST AND NEEDY

- "And if anyone gives so much as a cup of cold water to one of these little ones . . . that [person] will . . . not go unrewarded." (Matthew 10:42, NRSV)

- I have read many stories of the Great Depression years when someone down and out would knock at the door of a farm house asking for food, and the farm women would go into their kitchens and get together a meal for absolute strangers.

  ❧ Welcomer of the Lost and Needy,
      You offer food and a kind smile to the hungry
      and comfort to those who have lost their way.
      Give us the wisdom to remember
      that the "strangers" could be us
          but for a quirk of fate:
      that, recalling your compassion,
      we give with generous hearts
          to those in need.

Woman who opens the door unafraid,
Beggarwoman,
You are Love who never grows weary.
Amen.

Fourteenth Sunday in Ordinary Time (July 3–9)

GIVER OF REST TO THE WEARY

- "Come to me, all whose work is hard, whose load is heavy; and I will give you relief. . . . Learn from me, for I am gentle and humble-hearted. . . . My yoke is good to bear, my load is light." (Matthew 11:28–30, NRSV)
- In Guatamala and many other countries the indigenous (Mayan) women and even young girls carry large bundles of goods for the market on their heads from place to place. I have never seen one of these women, even on rough cobblestone, take a misstep or lose her balance. I understand, however, that occasionally a woman's neck will break under the weight of her burden.

> ❧ Giver of Rest to the Weary,
> gently You take the loads from the backs of the
>   poor
> and offer support to those who feel they can go
>   no farther.
> Teach us to share the burdens of one another:
> that, recognizing our interdependence,
> we accept responsibility for ourselves and all people;
> WomanChrist beside us,
> WomanChrist beyond us,
> You are Christ-within-Us forever. Amen.

Fifteenth Sunday in Ordinary Time (July 10–16)

CONVENER OF THE QUILTING BEE

- "And some of the seed fell into good soil, where it bore fruit, yielding a hundredfold or, it might be sixtyfold or thirtyfold. . . . For the [one] who has will be given more, till [that person] has enough and to spare." (Matthew 13:8–9, 12, NRSV)

   ❧ Convenor of the Quilting Bee,
     You call us into fellowship with You
        and one another,
     and invite us to stitch our lives into the quilt
        of your unfolding.
     Inspire us with your design
     in which heaven and earth are filled with your justice:
     that, with You, we gather the remnants of the nations
        into one people,
     and participate in the piecing together of your New
        Creation.
     Great Seamstress,
     Fabric of Life,
     the thread of your steadfast love joins us to You
        and all the Universe. Amen.

Sixteenth Sunday in Ordinary Time (July 17–23)

LOVER OF WEEDS

- The dualism in Matthew 13:24–30, 36–43 splits humankind into the "chosen" and the "unchosen," and the world into "God's realm" and "the realm of the Devil," distorting the proper image of the universe as God's body, a universe which is an organic whole, a totality of all its parts.[60]

- As a small child I found great joy in wildflowers. I would carry my bouquet into the house, and my father would say, "All they

are is weeds." His opinion never dampened my enthusiasm for
seeking out the wild beauty of nature's bounty.

❧ Lover of Weeds,
    You created the wildflowers
        and the beasts of the field.
    From your Body, the Universe,
    evolved all living things,
    and there is no creature in heaven or earth
        whom You do not love.
    Teach us the Wisdom of valuing all of life:
    that, leaving behind the dualisms of worlds past,
    we enter into unity with You and all Creation;
    Spiritwoman who draws all into one,
    You are our Living Body,
    and our World without End. Amen.

Seventeenth Sunday in Ordinary Time (July 24–30)

FIELD OF HEAVEN AND EARTH

- "The kingdom of Heaven is like treasure hidden in a field which
  someone has found; he hides it again, goes off in his joy, sells
  everything he owns and buys it." (Matthew 13:44–46, NJB)

❧ Field of Heaven and Earth,
    You invite us into yourself to grow in love
        with You and all creatures:
    the purple thistle, the milkweed, the stinging nettle
        and the katydid,
    fossils embedded in the soil, shells from an
        ancient sea,
    and the ladybug sunning on a blade of grass.
    Open our heart to the wonders of your nature:
    that, loving the earth as our own bodies,
        every nook and cranny,

we become one with You in bringing all things
into the perfect health of your blessing.
Meadow of Our Delight,
Vineyard of Our Desire,
the ground of your compassion sustains us forever.
Amen.

Eighteenth Sunday in Ordinary Time (July 31–August 6)

FISH WHO SWIMS THE SEA

- "[Jesus] told the people to sit down on the grass; then, taking the
  five loaves and the two fishes, he . . . said the blessing, broke the
  loaves . . . , and the disciples gave them to the people. They all
  ate to their hearts' content." (Matthew 14:19–20, NRSV)

  Fish who Swims in the Sea,
  You dwell in waters which cannot drown
  and give your body to nourish the hungry.
  Feed us with the compassion of Jesus:
  that, like You, we willingly give our lives
  for the health and wholeness of the Universe.
  Embryonic Waters,
  Bread of Heaven,
  You are the Flow of Eternal Life. Amen.

Prayers after Pentecost:
Womangod as Queen of the Universe
— ❧ —

(Sundays in Ordinary Time, August 7–October 8)

Nineteenth Sunday of Ordinary Time (August 7–13)

SISTER OF THE ELEMENTS

- "Immediately [Jesus] made the disciples get into the boat and go on ahead to the other side, while he dismissed the crowds. . . . When evening came . . . by this time the boat, battered by the waves, was far from the land, for the wind was against them. And early in the morning he came walking toward them on the sea. . . . 'Take heart, it is I; do not be afraid.'" (Matthew 14:22–27, NRSV)

- "[Elijah] was told, 'Go out and stand on the mountain before Yahweh.' Then Yahweh himself went by. There came a mighty wind, so strong it tore the mountains and shattered the rocks before Yahweh. But Yahweh was not in the wind." (1 Kings 19:11, JB)

❧ Sister of the Elements,
tempests do not frighten You,
and the waves of the sea do not overcome You.
Show us how we are connected with your creation,
and turn us from self-centeredness to respect
for each particle of this planet:

that, calming the chaos of our own spirits,
we learn to soothe earth's stormy outbursts.
Strongwoman who hugs the Universe to her bosom,
Embodied One,
You are the Lioness who lies down with the Lamb.
Amen.

Twentieth Sunday of Ordinary Time (August 14–20)

WOMAN WHO ASKS FOR WHAT SHE NEEDS

- "a Canaanite woman . . . came out and started shouting, 'Have mercy on me, Lord, Son of David; my daughter is tortured by a demon.' He answered, 'I was sent only to the lost sheep of the house of Israel.' But she came and knelt before him, saying, 'Lord, help me . . . even the dogs eat the crumbs that fall from their masters' table.' Then Jesus answered her, 'Woman, great is your faith! Let it be done for you as you wish.'" (Matthew 15:22–28, NRSV)

- "God has imprisoned all [humanity] in their own disobedience only to show mercy to all [people]." (Romans 11:32, JB)

     ❧ Assertive Woman,
        You do not hesitate to ask for what You need
            for your children,
        and You persist in the face of opposition.
        Teach us to speak out for justice
        and to refuse to allow others to decide
            what our place is:
        that, claiming our dignity before You
            and humankind,
        we enter with You into the salvation of Shalom.
        Courageous Grandmother,
        Liberating Goddess,
        You are the Spirit of Righteousness. Amen.

Twenty-First Sunday of Ordinary Time (August 21–27)

GODDESS OF MARTHA

- "Simon Peter answered, 'You are the Messiah, the Son of the living God.' And Jesus answered him, 'Blessed are you, Simon son of Jonah. . . . I tell you, you are Peter, and on this rock I will build my church.'" (Matthew 16:16–18, NRSV)

See Lent 5, GODDESS OF MARTHA, for the female equivalent in the Gospels of Peter's confession.

MOTHER OF WISDOM

- "There was . . . a woman of Levi. . . . She conceived and gave birth to a son and, seeing what a fine child he was, she kept him hidden for three months. When she could hide him no longer, she got a papyrus basket for him; coating it with bitumen and pitch, she put the child inside and laid it among the reeds at the river's edge." (Exodus 2:1–3, JB)

ॐ Sweet Shaddai,
   You gave the mother of Moses a passion for life
      that brought forth wisdom
   and sent the girl Miriam on her heroic quest
      to save the life of her brother.
   Incite us with your maternal compassion for all
      children whose lives are in danger:
   that, setting aside our need to save ourselves,
   we work with courage to bring about justice
      for all people.
   Breastfeeding Woman,
   Innocent One,
   You are the Spirit who brings liberation
      to the nations
   and sweeps us into kinship with You. Amen.

GODDESS OF SHIPRAH AND PUAH

- "But the midwives were God-fearing: they disobeyed the command of the king of Egypt and let the boys live. So the king . . . summoned the midwives. 'Why . . . have you . . . spared the boys?' 'The Hebrew women are not like Egyptian women,' they answered Pharaoh, 'they are hardy, and they give birth before the midwife reaches them.'" (Exodus 1:17–20, JB)

 ᕔ Divine Midwife,
   in Shiprah and Puah You defied the tyranny of
       Pharoah
   and subverted the cruelty of the social order.
   Fill us with your passion for life:
   that we, too, stand strong in the face of oppression.
   Guide in the Dark Night of the Soul,
   Hands that move us gently Home,
   You are the One Who Enables Us to pass from fear
       into the courage of unity with You,
   Triune Goddess forever. Amen.

Twenty-Second Sunday of Ordinary Time
(August 28–September 3)

PEASANT WOMAN

- "From that time on, Jesus began to show his disciples that he must go to Jerusalem and undergo great suffering at the hands of the elders and chief priests and scribes, and be killed, and on the third day be raised." (Matthew 16:21, NRSV)

- When my spouse returned from his role with the World Council of Churches observing the election runoffs in El Salvador, he brought me a small cross on which, curiously, or not so curiously, rather than a male Jesus, was painted a peasant woman. The woman's arms were flung wide, and in the background were other peasant women in a village setting. Peasant women as well as men have been the victims of death squads in Guatamala and El Salvador both as innocent bystanders and as activists in the struggle to achieve justice for their people.

ᑐ Peasant Woman,
  You are cast out of your hut,
      beaten and tortured
  for no more reason than that You loved
      your children
  and longed for a future in which justice
      is done.
  By your death testify to us of your love
      for the poor and the oppressed:
  that, awakened from our complacency,
  we seek with You to bring peace to the earth.
  Old Grandmother who sees all,
  Crucified One,
  You are the Spirit who longs to heal her children.
  Amen.

For the Revised Common Lectionary reading on Exodus 3:1–5, see ONE WHO MAKES THE GROUND HOLY, Trinity Sunday, in Volume B (1993) of *Seasons of the Feminine Divine.*

EAGLEWOMAN

- "On the third new moon after the Israelites had gone out of the land of Egypt, on that very day, they came into the wilderness of Sinai." (Exodus 19:1, NRSV)

- "You have seen what I did to the Egyptians, and how I bore you on eagles' wings and brought you to myself. Now, therefore, if you obey my voice and keep my covenant, you shall be my treasured possession . . . a holy nation." (Exodus 19:4–6, NRSV)

ᑐ Eaglewoman,
  on your great wing You bear us up,
  carrying us to the place where You know
      we will be safe.

Help us to remember the freedom
You have given us:
that, remaining faithful to You and one another,
we do not fall again into the slavery of oppression.
Falcon of the Third Moon,
One of Strength and Vision,
You fly to us in mercy. Amen.

Twenty-Third Sunday of Ordinary Time (September 4–10)

DIVINE EAR

- "Again . . . I tell you, if two of you agree on earth about anything you ask, it will be done for you by my Father in heaven.
  For where two or three are gathered in my name, I am there
  among them." (Matthew 18:19–20, NRSV)

- Divine Ear,
  You hear the cries of your creatures
  and welcome us when we appeal to You.
  Enable us to tune in to the lives of others:
  that, entering the labyrinth of their need,
  we whisper the words of hope
  that You have given us.
  Mother who listens for her children,
  Sound of Human Longing,
  You are the Channel through whom we dare
      to dream. Amen.

FIERY MOUNTAIN

- "On the morning of the third day there was thunder and light-
  ning, as well as a thick cloud on the mountain, and a blast of
  a trumpet so loud that all the people who were in the camp
  trembled. . . . Now Mount Sinai was wrapped in smoke,
  because the Lord had descended upon it in fire; the smoke

went up like the smoke of a kiln, while the whole mountain shook violently. . . . The Lord summoned Moses to the top of the mountain, and Moses went up." (Exodus 19:16–20, NRSV)

- Standing on the side of a great volcano in Costa Rica, far out of reach of the lava that sprayed from its mouth and feeling the rumbling of the ground beneath me, I felt the tremendous power of the earth beyond anything I ever imagined possible!

❧ Fiery Mountain,
    You release the excess of energy
        from the center of the earth,
    and spill molten rock to fertilize the valleys.
    Awe us with the splendor of your creative power:
    that we not underestimate your capacity for good
    and seek with You to bring the world
        to equity and peace.
    El Shaddai, Earth Mother,
    Movable and Immovable One,
    You are the Headland of the Wisdom of the Ages,
    Blessed Trinity now and forever. Amen.

Twenty-Fourth Sunday of Ordinary Time (September 11–17)

QUEEN OF THE DEAD AND THE LIVING

- "If we live, we live to the Lord, and if we die, we die to the Lord; so then, whether we live or whether we die, we are the Lord's. For to this end Christ died and lived again, so that he might be Lord of both the dead and the living." (Romans 14:8–9, NRSV)

- "Then Peter came and said to [Jesus], 'Lord, if another member of the church sins against me, how often should I forgive? As many as seven times?' Jesus said to him, 'Not seven times, but I tell you, seventy times seven.'" (Matthew 18:21–22, NRSV)

๛ Queen of the Dead and the Living,
     there is no place where we can leave the sphere
          of your mercy,
     and no deed which You cannot move through
          your pain to forgive.
     Open our hearts to receive the grace of Christ
          crucified:
     that, repenting of the ways we promote discord
          and injustice,
     we turn to live out our lives in kinship with You.
     One Who Inhabits Our Darkness,
     Bringer of the Light,
     You gather all creation into unity with You forever.
     Amen.

Twenty-Fifth Sunday of Ordinary Time (September 18–24)

BENEVOLENT EMPLOYER

- "For the kingdom of heaven is like a landowner who went out early in the morning to hire laborers for his vineyard. . . . Now when the first [laborers] came, they thought they would receive more; but each of them also received the usual daily wage. And . . . they grumbled against the landowner. . . . But he replied to them, 'Friend, I am doing you no wrong; did you not agree with me for the usual daily wage? Take what belongs to you and go. . . . So the last will be first, and the first will be last." (Matthew 20:1–16, NSRV)

๛ Benevolent Employer,
     You surprise us when You do not behave as we
          expect,
     and challenge us to rethink what we have taken
          for granted.
     Give us the wisdom to discern the parts of our
          traditions You call us to leave behind,
     and to hold fast to those things that are essential:

that, trusting in your guidance, we move by faith
　　into that Land
where the first are last and the last first.
Dame Wisdom,
Toiler in the Unfolding of the Cosmos,
You are Spiritwoman who opens the way to new
　　vistas, even to the end of time. Amen.

LAMENT ON THE DESTRUCTION OF THE GODDESS IMAGE IN THE JUDEO-CHRISTIAN TRADITION

- "When the people saw that Moses delayed to come down from the mountain, [they] gathered around Aaron [who] said to them, 'Take off the gold rings that are on the ears of your wives, your sons, and your daughters, and bring them to me.' ... He took the gold from them, formed it in a mold, and cast an image of a calf; and they said, 'These are your gods, O Israel, who brought you up out of the land of Egypt!' ... The Lord said to Moses, 'Go down at once! Your people ... have acted perversely.'" (Exodus 32:1-7, NRSV)

- "When Moses saw that the people were running wild, [he] stood in the gate of the camp, and said, 'Who is on the Lord's side?' and all the sons of Levi gathered around him. He said to them, 'Thus says the Lord, the God of Israel, 'Put your sword on your side, each of you! Go back and forth from gate to gate throughout the camp, and each of you kill your brother, your friend, and your neighbor.' ... and about three thousand of the people fell on that day." (Exodus 32:25-28, NRSV)

- "... when Solomon was old, his wives turned away his heart after other gods; and his heart was not true to the Lord his God, as was the heart of his father David. For Solomon followed Astarte the goddess of the Sidonians, and Milcom the abomination of the Ammonites. ... Then the Lord was angry ... [and] ... said, 'Since this has been your mind and you have not kept my covenant and my statutes that I have commanded you, I will surely tear the kingdom from you and give it to your servant.'" (1 Kings 11:1-11, NRSV)

- Jezebel and Athaliah, among others, are depicted as evil women in the biblical narrative, and certainly a case is made for this portrayal; yet, from the perspective of those defending their ancient religions against the violent onslaught of the Israelites, one wonders if there could be another side to their stories.

🙟 Wanton One of Israel,
Birth-giver, Source of Creation,
You were once the focus of divine identity.
You contained us in the dark safety of your belly,
and brought us to birth through the fertile redness
    of your woman-cycle;
By the milk of your breasts You gave us life.

In ancient times You made yourself known in the form of
    Womangod
and spoke to humankind through the wonders of your
    creativity.
You arose in the consciousness of the people as
    Woman Elder,
as the Wise One who oversaw the care of her people,
and took form in the human imagination as the
    thousand-named-Goddess:
Astarte, Asherah, Isis, and others.
For a time You lived in the wisdom of Rebekah who made
    the last first, according to your will;
in Rachel's pouch You pursued us into the wilderness
    of the new religion.
You revealed your strength in the military prowess of
    Deborah and the savage expedience of Jael.

But then You turned from us and no longer looked
    on us with favor.
When You saw Miriam, radiant with the sweat of
    frenzied dance,

You struck her white with leprosy;
You hid your face from her and let her be driven from
    holy history.
Within a few short years women were subdued and passive:
    mothers filled with docility, women of cunning who
    manipulated those in power,
Bathsheba summoned on command to the bed of the king,
    Esther able to save her people only through beauty
    and submission.
Your last queens, Athaliah and Jezebel, were objectified
    as evil and murdered;
even Solomon bore the contempt of the elders
    because of his respect for your daughters of strength.

Yet, when You allowed yourself to be subdued
    by the sons of Abraham,
You left us stranded and without power.
Though we searched for You in the high places
where we had once worshipped You freely and with joy,
    we did not find You;
we witnessed your repeated rape in the destruction
    of the statues that had symbolized your Presence;
we heard echoes of the cries of our sisters, Dinah, Tamar,
    and women through the ages.
Like Lillith You flew from us,
leaving us with the confusion of Eve.

They turned against You in your maternal manifestation;
they called You evil, the despoiler of souls!
They enslaved those who bore your form,
and proclaimed your sacred powers unclean!
They campaigned against your priestesses, and called
    them prostitutes;
they slaughtered and stoned and burned them to death.
Generation after generation they destroyed You;

women lived in fear of being named your own!
They erased your womanly name from the surface of
    the earth;
no one, not one daughter, remembered the goodness of
    your aspect!

We weep, O Goddess, at the length of your absence;
for a thousand years we have longed for your return;
we have moaned and torn our hair,
not knowing who it was that we cried for,
nor who it is who can give us back ourselves,
    fragrant with your holiness.
Where can we go to re-discover You?
Who can illumine our hearts with stories of your love?
Who can explain the gentleness of your caress,
    or the sweetness of your call?
Sing to us in the breeze that ripples through the trees
    in the apple orchards,
the wind that swoops up the mountain sides,
the gusts that skim like a smooth stone atop the
waves that undulate to the song of the sea!
Greet us with the tenderness of a Lover who knows
the intensity of our desire and the inner character of
    our sorrowing.

Yet, unknown to us, You have stolen alongside us
    and guided us through the wasteland of our
    destruction.
You lurked in the wisdom of the ages,
 pointing us beyond the obvious to the obscure hope of
    renewal and new life.
You were the well-kept secret of the cherubim,
    hidden in the bowels of the holy of holies.
You spoke in the voice of the prophets who challenged
    the legalism and hard-heartedness of their day,

and called once more to centrality the power of your
  womb-love:
  steadfast and merciful.
At the right time You entered the soul of Jesus,
  and gave him a heart of love for all people.
You arose once more in the memory of his mother, Mary,
and excited the imaginations of Christians for generations.
Mother Jesus,
Sophia-Christ,
the prophecy of your Spirit sustains us forever!
Amen.

Twenty-Sixth Sunday in Ordinary Time
(September 25–October 1)

LADY SHEKINAH

- "[The Lord] said, 'My presence will go with you, and I will give you rest. . . . See, there is a place by me where you shall stand on the rock; and while my glory passes by I will put you in a cleft of the rock, and I will cover you with my hand until I have passed by.'" (Exodus 33:14, 21–22)

- "What do you think? A man had two sons; he went to the first and said, 'Son go and work in the vineyard today.' He answered, 'I will not'; but later he changed his mind and went. . . . The second . . . answered, 'I go, sir'; but he did not go. Which of the two did the will of his father? . . . Truly I tell you, the tax collectors and the prostitutes are going into the kingdom of God ahead of you." (Matthew 21:28–31, NRSV)

- My two children behaved in exactly the ways described in this parable; yet I cannot say that I love one less than the other; they are both treasures in my heart.

  ❧ Lady Shekinah,
      You cover the earth with your glory
      and call each of us by name.

You set us in a safe place
and cover us with your hand.
Open our hearts to your loving kindness:
that, sustained by your eternal nearness,
we go out into the world with confidence.
Numinous Presence,
You are the Radiance of the Angels,
the Promise of Forgiveness,
and the One who dwells in us for all time. Amen.

Twenty-Seventh Sunday in Ordinary Time (October 2–8)

GODDESS AS LANDOWNER

- "There was a landowner who planted a vineyard, put a fence around it, dug a wine press in it, and built a watchtower. Then he . . . went to another country. When the harvest time had come, he sent his slaves to the tenants to collect his produce. But the tenants seized his slaves and beat one, killed another, and stoned another. . . . Finally he sent his son to them, saying, 'They will respect my son.' But when the tenants saw the son . . . they seized him, threw him out of the vineyard and killed him." (Matthew 21:33–39, NRSV)

  Owner of the Earth,
    You reach out in mercy and justice
    to make this planet wholesome and life-giving.
    Yet we exploit your resources for our own purposes;
    forgetting the poor, we imagine our positions
        of privilege as your reward.
    Confront us with the judgment of floundering
        economies and the loss of wealth:
    that, forced into modes of survival,
    we recognize the poor and oppressed as our sisters
        and brothers.
    One Who Awaits the Harvest,

Beggarwoman who gleans the fields,
You are the Spirit who scorches the earth with
    the fire of your sighs,
Triune Goddess, forever. Amen.

Harvest Thanksgiving

MOTHER OF THE GOOD EARTH

- "For the Lord your God is bringing you into a good land, a land with flowing streams, a land of wheat and barley, of vines and fig trees and pomegranates, a land of olive trees and honey, a land where you may eat bread without scarcity, where you will lack nothing. . . . When you have eaten your fill . . . then do not exalt yourself, forgetting the Lord your God, who brought you out of the land of Egypt . . . who led you through...an arid wasteland with poisonous snakes and scorpions . . . and fed you . . . with manna." (Deuteronomy 8:7–16, NRSV)

❧ Mother of the Good Earth,
You flood the land with fresh water
and bring to harvest wheat and barley,
    vines and fig trees,
pomegranates succulent with the nectar of your love.
Teach us to remember You in seasons
    of prosperity,
and to trust You when we are in want:
that at all times we give generously to every
    one in need
and reap the bounty of Shalom our home;
One Who Stays the Bite of the Fiery Snake,
Giver of Manna,
You are the Stream of Unending Love.
Amen.

Prayers after Pentecost:
One Who Brings Us Home

— ∾ —

(Sundays in Ordinary Time, October 9–November 26)

Twenty-Eighth Sunday in Ordinary Time (October 9–15)

GODDESS OF EUODIA AND SYNTYCHE

- "I urge Euodia and . . . Syntyche to be of the same mind in the Lord . . . for they have struggled beside me in the work of the gospel, together with Clement and the rest of my co-workers, whose names are in the book of life." (Philippians 4:2–3, NRSV)

∾ One who Struggles with Us,
   You gave strength and authority to Euodia and
      Syntyche,
   co-workers with Paul in taking the gospel of
      your love to the world.
   In times of conflict in the Christian community,
   remind us of our common purpose in Christ:
   that, working out our differences with respect for
      one another,
   we come to know in fullness your peace that
      passes understanding.
   Wisdom of the Ages,
   Sister of Strong Conviction,

You are the Spirit who calls us to reconciliation
and wholeness.
Amen.

FRIEND OF THE HOMELESS

- "Then [the king] said, . . . 'The wedding is ready, but those
invited were not worthy. Go therefore into the main streets,
and invite everyone you find to the wedding banquet.'"
(Matthew 22:8–9, NRSV)

❧ Friend of the Homeless,
    You know what it is like to have no place to lay
        your head,
    nor certainty that there is a meal for You at the
        end of day.
    Give us the wisdom to find You in those who are
        destitute:
    that, caring for people who are forgotten and
        outcast,
    we participate in bringing humanity into oneness
        with You forever.
    Creatress of Humankind,
    Divine Beggarwoman,
    You feed the world with your Love. Amen.

Twenty-Ninth Sunday in Ordinary Time (October 16 –22)
To Karen

WOMAN TAX COLLECTOR

- "'Teacher, we know that you are sincere, and teach the way of
God in accordance with truth, and show deference to no one;
for you do not regard people with partiality. Tell us, then, what
you think. Is it lawful to pay taxes to the emperor, or not?' But
Jesus, aware of their malice, said, 'Why are you putting me to

the test, you hypocrites? . . . Give . . . to the emperor the things
that are the emperor's, and to God the things that are God's.'"
(Matthew 22:16–21, NRSV)

🙌 Auditor of the Human Heart,
You inspect the record of our lives
and gently probe the motives of our actions.
Open the book of our soul
to the warmth of your concern:
that every item that turns us from You
be erased from our account,
and we live with You and one another
in the treasure house of your Love;
One Who Seeks to Know Us,
Friend Who Listens,
You are Wisdom who gives clarity
        to our lives. Amen.

ONE WHO CALLS US INTO JOURNEY

• ". . . Naomi said to her two daughters-in-law, 'Go back each of
you to your mother's house. May the Lord deal kindly with you,
as you have dealt with the dead and with me. The Lord grant
that you may find security, each of you in the house of your husband.' Then she kissed them, and they wept aloud. . . . But Ruth
said, 'Do not press me to leave you. . . . Where you go, I will
go.'" (Ruth 1:8–16, NRSV)

🙌 One Who Calls Us into Journey with You,
You spoke to Ruth through the love of Naomi,
and gave her the courage to follow You,
        the God with breasts.[61]
Bless our relationships with one another,
that nurtured in your community of faith,
our lives become gifts of your mercy to the
        world;
Glorious Shaddai, You are the Holy One forever.
Amen.

LAMENT FOR WOMEN REFUGEES

   ᔰ Ancient Woman,
     when You feel the shadow fall across the land,
     and hear the sound of trudging on unyielding roadbeds,
     and against the roughness of jungle paths,
     where is your heart?
     When You see women's feet,
     shoes left far behind in pieces among the jagged rocks,
     blood crusting over gashes, bruises, welts,
     over callused skin cracking with the dryness of hot sun,
     marching in cadence to the thin wailing of infants
        outraged from hunger
     and from mothers' breasts that no longer have the strength
        to feed,
     what do You feel?
     And when the tiny voices fall silent,
     and still the women plod, clutching small corpses
        to their chests,
     as silently, one by one, they sink into the bush
        at the side of the road,
     too weary to weep or be afraid,
     too tired to care about anything anymore,
     do You notice? Do You care?

     We notice, fleetingly, the tragedy,
     seen distantly on our television screens.
     We reach out to help in small, inadequate ways,
     a reasonable donation through a local charity —
     while You — You know how many hairs
        are upon each head.
     You feel every nuance of pain in their sojourn to death,
     each gasp for one more breath.

     No one counts the numbers of the ones who slide
        to the ground
     to be clasped in death into your motherly embrace.

No one perceives the agonized ripping of your
     earthen heart;
the heaving of sobbing clay goes unheard.

Old Woman,
You have seen many misfortunes along the human journey.
Open our hearts to the plight of the refugees,
for women and men who suffer from no more reason
     than the coincidence of geography.
Open our hearts to the lovers of justice and the defenders
     of human rights,
the ones who have heeded the ring of the phone,
obeyed the whispered warning,
survived the dash by car in the dark of night
to cross the border not a moment too soon —
the ones who have lived and did not die as the others did,
     tortured, bludgeoned, disappeared.
Open our hearts, Holy One, to those who are uprooted
     and in need of a place to stay:
that with You we advance the clock of time to your
     Resurrection Day,
when all will live with You and one another in friendship
     and peace forever! Amen.

All Saints' Day

GATHERER OF ALL GOOD MEMORIES

- "Gathered together am I, from a history-held mystery, a bun-
  dle of memories am I . . . the blessing of eternity passed on:
  urgency always to seek the face of God, first gatherer of all
  good memories."[62]
- "Treasured memories are waiting there deep within me. As I
  recall them, I will be able to see my life filled with daily mira-
  cles, fashioning my heart into a vessel of gratitude."[63]

❧ Gatherer of All Good Memories,
   You are a treasure house of joy that sustains
      and empowers us.
   When we are discouraged,
   remind us of the times when You have come to us
      in our friends,
   in our sisters and brothers,
   our grandmothers and even strangers:
   that, filled with gratitude,
   we are strengthened to love and nurture your
      creation
   and witness to the wholeness of the Universe in You
      forever. Amen.

Thirtieth Sunday in Ordinary Time (October 23–29)

HEART OF THE UNIVERSE

- "'You shall love the Lord your God with all your heart, and
  with all your soul, and with all your mind.' This is the great-
  est and first commandment. And a second is like it: 'You shall
  love your neighbor as yourself.'" (Matthew 22:37–39, NRSV)

- ". . . We could have imposed ourselves on you with full weight.
  . . . Instead, we were unassuming. Like a mother feeding and
  looking after her own children, we felt so devoted and protective toward you, and had come to love you so much, that we
  were eager to hand over to you not only the Good News but
  our whole lives as well." (1 Thessalonians 2:7–8, JB)

❧ Heart of the Universe,
   when we weep, You contract in pain,
   and when we are afraid, You fill Us
      with strength and energy.
   Empower us to live out our passion for You:
   that, through the mothering of others,

we mirror the reflection of your Love for the
    world.
For You are the Source of our vitality,
the Center of our innermost selves,
and the Courage of our convictions,
Womangod One-in-Three forever. Amen.

Thirty-First Sunday in Ordinary Time
(October 30–November 5)

WOMAN BEARING THE BURDEN OF THE WORLD

- ["Jesus said . . . 'The scribes and the Pharisees sit on Moses'
  seat; therefore, do whatever they teach you and follow it; but
  do not do as they do, for they do not practice what they teach.
  They tie up heavy burdens, hard to bear, and lay them on the
  shoulders of others; but they themselves are unwilling to lift a
  finger to move them." (Matthew 23:1–4, NRSV)

    Woman Bearing the Burden of the World,
    You creep from your hovel long before daylight
    to clean the houses of the wealthy;
    from the lingering warmth of their hearthstones
    You scrub soot and ashes.
    Teach us to use our riches to heal the minds
        and bodies of the destitute:
    that, giving up our places of privilege,
    we lift the weight of oppression
        from the world.
    Porter of the Gate of Life,
    Messenger of Hope,
    You are Eaglewoman who transports us
    on her wings of grace into the joy of Shalom.
    Amen.

For Amos 5:18–24, see WOMANGOD AS LIONESS, Thirty-Second Sunday in Ordinary Time (November 6–12).

DIVINE MATCHMAKER

- "Naomi [Ruth's mother-in-law] said to her, 'My daughter, I need to seek some security for you, so that it may be well with you. . . . Now wash and anoint yourself, and put on your best clothes and go down to the threshing floor; but do not make yourself known to the man until he has finished eating and drinking. When he lies down, observe the place . . . then, go and uncover his feet and lie down; and he will tell you what to do." (Ruth 3:1–5, NRSV)

  ✌ Divine Matchmaker,
  You paired Ruth's daring with Boaz' compassion,
  and welcomed a foreigner into the family of
      David.
  Open our hearts to love people who are not like us:
  that, blessed with their enrichment of our lives,
  we may be blessings to others in Christ's name.
  Sagacious Old Woman,
  Song of Love,
  You are Heart that gives life to the Universe. Amen.

Thirty-Second Sunday in Ordinary Time (November 6–12)

OIL OF GLADNESS

- "Ten bridesmaids took their oil and went to meet the bridegroom. . . . The wise took flasks of oil with their lamps. . . . The foolish said to the wise, 'Give us some of your oil, for our lamps are going out.' But the wise replied, 'No! There will not be enough for you and for us. . . . And while they went to buy [oil] . . . those who were ready went with [the bridegroom] into the wedding banquet; and the door was shut." (Matthew 25:1–10, NRSV)

- "The spirit of the Lord God is upon me, because the Lord has
anointed me; he has sent me to bring good news to the
oppressed, to bind up the brokenhearted, to proclaim liberty
to the captives, and release to the prisoners . . . to comfort all
who mourn . . . to give them a garland instead of ashes, the oil
of gladness instead of mourning." (Isaiah 61:1–3, NRSV)

🙚 Oil of Gladness,
 You soothe us with your touch
 and make us the resource of your availability
  to the sick,
 the discouraged, and the brokenhearted.
 Exhilarate us with the aroma of your earthiness,
  — cinnamon-bark, pimiento or wintergreen —:
 that, strengthened by your sustaining presence,
 we become the agent of your healing of pain
  and injustice.
 Well from the Center of the Earth,
 Illuminator,
 You moisten the brittleness of our souls. Amen.

LIONESS OF THE VELDT

- "Alas for you who desire the day of the Lord! . . . It is darkness, not light, as if someone fled from a lion, and was met by
a bear." (Amos 5:18–19, NRSV)

- "For the Lord . . . with a cry of command, with the archangel's
call and with the sound of God's trumpet, will descend from
heaven. . . . Then we...will be caught up in the clouds together with [the dead in Christ] . . . and so we will be with the Lord
forever." (1 Thessalonians 4:13–18, NRSV).

- "Lions were known in Palestine during Biblical times. . . . The
female . . . lioness . . . weighing about three hundred pounds
. . . travels alone or in a group, called a pride . . . most of the
killing and hunting is done by the females. Very crafty, the lion
always stalks prey under cover of darkness. . . . Unlike other

beasts of prey, the lion shares its kill. . . . the cubs are born in a nest prepared in a thicket or a cave in the rocks . . . [and they are] in their mother's care for at least a year."[64]

☙ Lioness of the Veldt[65] of Our Terror,
  when we flee your day of judgment,
  You spring after us;
  your speed is too much for us.
  Ensnare us in the nest You have prepared for us:
  that, astonished by your motherly tenderness,
  we live with You forever in the thicket
      of your dwelling place.
  Wisdom from the East,
  Ancient Prowler of Palestine,
  You are Womanspirit who nurtures her young.
  Amen.

For 1 Thessalonians 5:1–11 see also WOMAN BANKER, Thirty-Third Sunday in Ordinary Time (November 13–19).

Thirty-Third Sunday in Ordinary Time (November 13–19)

WOMAN BANKER

• "'You wicked and lazy slave! You knew . . . that I reap where I did not sow, and gather where I did not scatter? Then you ought to have invested my money with the bankers, and on my return I would have received what was my own with interest.'" (Matthew 25:26–27, NRSV).

☙ Woman Banker,
  You overturn the tills of your place
      of business,
  and share your revenue with the lost
      and destitute.

Upset the economies of our souls:
that, turning from the materialism
that usurps the passion of our hearts,
we labor with You in the creation
        of a just society
in which all people reverence You in one another.
Steward of the Universe,
One who gives us what is yours,
You are our treasure forever. Amen.

For Matthew 23:1–12, see Woman Bearing the Burden of the
World, Thirty-first Sunday in Ordinary Time (October
30–November 5).

Last Sunday after Pentecost: The Reign of Christ

SHEPHERDESS OF THE UNIVERSE

- "When the Son of Man comes in his glory . . . he will separate
  people one from another as a shepherd separates the sheep
  from the goats. . . . Then the king will say to those at his right
  hand, 'Come, you that are blessed by my Father, inherit the
  kingdom prepared for you from the foundation of the world;
  for I was hungry and you gave me food, I was thirsty and you
  gave me something to drink, I was a stranger and you welcomed me, I was sick and you took care of me, I was in prison
  and you visited me." (Matthew 25:31–36, NRSV)

- ❧ Shepherdess of the Universe,
    You come in Glory to provide for the peoples
        of the earth.
    Gather your lambs into your arms.
    Wash away each blemish with gentleness and
        mercy.

Carry us into the Land of your Shalom
where every tear is wiped away
and every pain and imperfection healed:
that we know the wonder of your Love
and celebrate with joy our life with You.
Caretaker of the Saved and the Lost,
One Who Knows Her Own by Name,
You are the Spirit Who Draws Creation
    into One with You forever;
Alleluia! Amen.

Notes

— 🕉 —

1. J. H. Otwell suggests that the title for the Divine, *Yahweh*, because of its feminine ending (the final *h*), is an abbreviated form of a longer title of a female deity. The particular form goes back to the fifth century B.C.E., whereas a longer form has been traced back as far as the fourteenth century B.C.E. While the short form appears to be used in the causative third person masculine singular ("He causes to come into being"), Otwell suggests that the history of the word makes "Lord" a feeble rendering of its meaning. *And Sarah Laughed* (Philadelphia: The Westminster Press, 1977), 188–89.

2. See Jeremiah 10:1–10.

3. Sally McFague, *Metaphorical Theology* (Philadelphia: Fortress Press, 1982), 11–12.

4. Edward J. Schmitt, *Moving to Meaning: Some Issues in Planning Based on Parish Vision* (Edmonton, Alberta: St. Stephen's College), 21–23. For more information concerning metaphor, see also, Northrop Frye, *The Great Code: The Bible and Literature* (Toronto: Academic Press Canada, 1982), 1–30; Paul Ricoeur, *The Rule of Metaphor: Multi-disciplinary Studies of the Creation of Meaning in Language*, trans. Robert Czerny (Toronto: University of Toronto Press, 1977), 193; Michael Polanyi and Harry Prosch, *Meaning* (Chicago: University of Chicago Press, 1975), 97; and Michael Polanyi, *Personal Knowledge: Towards a Post-Critical Philosophy* (Chicago: University of Chicago Press, 1958), 339.

5. Elaine Pagels, *The Gnostic Gospels* (New York: Random House, 1979), 48–69.

6. Ibid.; see also Elizabeth Schüssler Fiorenza, *In Memory of Her: A Feminist Theological Reconstruction of Christian Origins* (New York: Crossroad, 1984).

7. For an extended discussion of this view of nature, see Sally McFague, *The Body of God* (Minneapolis: Fortress Press, 1993), 26–64.

8. In *The Body of God*, McFague presents a detailed theology using the metaphor of the universe as the body of God.

9. Virginia Ramey Mollenkott, *Sensuous Spirituality: Out from Fundamentalism* (New York: Crossroad, 1992), 27. See also Neil Douglas-Klotz, *Prayers of the Cosmos: Meditations on the Aramaic Words of Jesus* (New York: Harper & Row, 1987).

10. Mollenkott, 16.

11. Carter Heyward, *Touching Our Strength: The Erotic as Power and the Love of God* (San Francisco: Harper & Row, 1989), 94.

12. Ibid., 90.

13. Phyllis Trible, *God and the Rhetoric of Sexuality* (Philadelphia: Fortress Press, 1978).

14. Mollenkott, 96–108.

15. Ibid., 96.

16. Heyward, 104–5.

17. Ibid., 98–99.

18. *Meditations with Julian of Norwich*, versions by Brendan Doyle (Santa Fe: Bear & Company, 1983), 29; as cited in Flora Slosson Wuellner, *Prayer and Our Bodies* (Nashville: The Upper Room, 1987), 40.

19. For insight into how the Hebrew word for "mercy" or "compassion" comes from the root word for "womb," and is translated "motherly-compassion" by Phyllis Trible, see her book *God and the Rhetoric of Sexuality* (Philadelphia: Fortress Press, 1978), 31–59.

20. See Joan Chamberlain, Engelsman, *The Feminine Dimension of the Divine* (Philadelphia: Westminster Press, 1979), 20–29.

21. Hadewijch of Brabant, "Mary, Mother of Love," in *Beguine Spirituality: an Anthology*, ed. Fiona Bowie (London: SPCK, 1989), 112.

22. To understand the use of the title "Goddess" here, see p. 18 in the introduction of *Seasons*, Cycle B, and p. 20 for reference to use of the title associated with Mary, the Mother of Jesus.

23. Hadewijch of Brabant, 125:

> Whatever gifts God bestowed upon us
> There was no one who could
> Understand true love
> Until Mary, in her goodness,
> And with deep humility,
> Received the gift of Love,
> She it was who tamed wild Love
> And gave us a lamb for a lion;
> Through her a light shone in the darkness
> That had endured so long.

24. Joyce Rupp, *The Star in My Heart: Experiencing Sophia, Inner Wisdom* (San Diego: Lura Media, 1990), 1–10.

25. Rafael Patai describes the Shekinah as having participated in the Exile with the Israelites, in their suffering and punishment, and also in their return. *The Hebrew Goddess* (Detroit: Wayne State University Press, 1990), 3rd ed., 154.

26. *The Random House Dictionary of the English Language*, College Edition, ed. Laurence Urdang (New York: Random House, 1968), 804.

27. Ibid., 1161.

28. See Leonard Swidler, *Biblical Affirmations of Woman* (Philadelphia: Westminster Press, 1979), 60–61, regarding the dove as symbol of the Holy Spirit but also of the Great Mother in ancient goddess worship.

29. The images in the ascription are drawn from Ilinor W. Gadon, *The Once and Future Goddess* (San Francisco: Harper & Row, 1989), 94. The dove represents the fullness of the Goddess as bearer of both life and death. She was also the emblem of Aphrodite/Venus, and, as Sophia, the soul of the Divine. The dove, as well, was the messenger of God to Noah and his family as she brought the olive branch and the assurance of the possibility of a new life ahead (Genesis 8:1–12).

30. Rather than submit to enslavement at the hands of the Spanish *conquistadores,* Mayan warriors hurled themselves over the cliffs of the Sumidero Canyon (state of Chiapas, Mexico).

31. Title from Kristin Weber, *WomanChrist: A New Vision of Feminist Spirituality* (San Francisco: Harper & Row, 1987).

32. Clark, Ronan, and Walker, *Image-Breaking Image-Building: A Handbook for Creative Worship with Women of Christian Tradition* (New York: The Pilgrim Press, 1981), 69.

33. For information regarding the scriptural basis for the mother bear image, see Virginia Mollenkott, The *Divine Feminine* (New York: Crossroad, 1984), 49–53.

34. See Jean Baker Miller, *Toward a Psychology of Women* (Boston: Beacon Press, 1976), 92, 99–102, 122–23; and Phyllis Chesler, *Women & Madness* (New York: Avon Books, 1972), 41–46. For a later and different view of anger in men and women, see Carol Tavris, *Anger: The Misunderstood Emotion* (New York: Simon & Schuster, 1982), 179–202. For an extensive exploration of women's anger, see Harriet Goldhor Lerner, *The Dance of Anger: A Woman's Guide to Changing the Patterns of Intimate Relationships* (New York: Harper & Row, 1985).

35. Title drawn from Lerner, *The Dance of Anger.*

36. Hadewijch of Brabant, 101.

37. The Shekinah was experienced as the numinous presence of God in the cloud that descended upon and dwelled within the desert tabernacle and subsequently Solomon's temple. It was the manifestation of this cloud that led the people of Israel through the wilderness. At night this Presence was made known in a pillar of

fire. She was understood to be a female presence. As well, in the earliest understanding of Yahweh, the Divine was thought to ride upon a chariot of cherubim or clouds; when these clouds settled on the tabernacle, it was like the wings of the cherubim folding down protectively. See Patai, 72–75, 96–97.

38. Rupp, v.

39. For an examination of the psychology of the image of "Enchanted Forest" see Rupp, 23–34.

40. Ibid., v.

41. Phrase drawn from hymn title "My Song Is Love Unknown," Godfrey Ridout, *The Hymn Book of the Anglican Church of Canada and the United Church of Canada*, Authorized by the General Synod and General Council 1 February 1971.

42. See M. Esther Harding, *Woman's Mysteries Ancient and Modern* (New York: Harper Colophon Books, Harper & Row, 1971), 84–97, for more information on the belief in ancient cultures that the moon had fertilizing powers.

43. For an interpretation of traditions around Martha, see Elisabeth Moltmann-Wendel, *The Women Around Jesus*, trans. John Bowden (London: SCM Press, 1982), 15–50.

44. For an interpretation of traditions around Mary Magdalene, see Moltmann-Wendel, 61–92.

45. Rupp, 35–46.

46. See Mollenkott, *The Divine Feminine*, 44–48 on the medieval symbol of Christ as Mother Pelican.

47. *The Random House Dictionary of the English Language*, ed. Laurence Urdang (New York: Random House, 1968), 1557.

48. For an interesting interpretation of the story of the woman who anointed Jesus, see Moltmann-Wendel, 93–98.

49. Eucharistic Prayer #5, *The Book of Alternative Services of the Anglican Church of Canada* (Toronto: Anglican Book Centre, 1985), 204.

50. Gabriele Uhlein, *Meditations with Hildegard of Bingen* (Santa Fe: Bear & Co., 1982).

51. See Rupp, 47–58, for her reflections on the value of positive memories.

52. The dove was the symbol of Aphrodite (Venus) and represented sexual passion and the soul returning to her after death, for she was understood as the bringer of death and peace. She represented the female soul of the Divine. In the Judeo-Christian tradition, the dove represented the Holy Spirit, an understanding of the Divine from Sophia/Hokmah (Wisdom) and from the concept of the shekinah or feminine presence of the Divine in the salvation story. Elinor W. Gadon, *The Once and Future Goddess* (San Francisco: Harper & Row, 1989), 94.

53. Patai, 154.

54. Kristen Weber, *WomanChrist*.

55. See Rupp, 59–68, regarding the image of Sophia inviting us to the window of new possibility.

56. See ibid., 1–10, for a description of the Spirit in the metaphor of star as our guide through our inner darkness.

57. Aritha van Herk, *Judith* (Toronto: McClellan and Stewart, 1978).

58. "Power-over" is a concept developed by Starhawk as a descriptive term for domination as compared to the power from within which is exercised for mutual care. *Dreaming the Dark: Magic, Sex & Politics* (Boston: Beacon Press, 1982), 1–14.

59. Ana Maria Rodas, *La Insurrection de Mariana* (Guatamala C.A.: Ediciones DEL CADEJO, 1993), 25. [Translation by the author]

60. See McFague, *The Body of God*, 27–64.

61. For more about El Shaddai, "the God with breasts," see Virginia Mollenkott, "The God of Naomi" in *The Divine Feminine* (New York: Crossroad, 1984), 54–59.

62. Rupp, 49.

63. Ibid., 57.

64. *Collier's Encyclopedia*, ed. William D. Halsey (New York: Crowell Collier and MacMillan, 1966), 14:675–76.

65. A *veldt* is the open brush and plains country of Africa and Asia where lions live.

Bibliography

— ❧ —

Anglican Church of Canada. *The Book of Alternative Services of the Anglican Church of Canada.* Toronto: Anglican Book Centre, 1985.

Clark, Linda, Marian Ronan, and Eleanor Walker. *Image-Breaking Image-Building: A Handbook for Creative Worship with Women of Christian Tradition.* New York: The Pilgrim Press, 1981.

Collier's Encyclopedia, ed. William D. Halsey. Vol. 14. New York: Crowell Collier and MacMillan, 1966.

Douglas-Klotz, Neil. *Prayers of the Cosmos: Meditations on the Aramaic Words of Jesus.* New York: Harper & Row, 1987.

Doyle, Brendan. *Meditations with Julian of Norwich.* Santa Fe: Bear & Company, 1983.

Engelsman, Joan Chamberlain. *The Feminine Dimension of the Divine.* Philadelphia: The Westminster Press, 1979.

Frye, Northrop. *The Great Code: The Bible and Literature.* Toronto: Academic Press Canada, 1982.

Gadon, Elinor W. *The Once and Future Goddess.* San Francisco: Harper & Row, 1989.

Hadewijch of Brabant. "Mary, Mother of Love." In Fiona Bowie, ed. *Beguine Spirituality: An Anthology.* London: SPCK, 1989.

Harding, Esther. *Woman's Mysteries Ancient and Modern.* New York: Harper & Row, 1971.

Heyward, Carter. *Touching Our Strength: The Erotic as Power and the Love of God.* San Francisco: Harper & Row, 1989.

Lerner, Harriet Goldhor. *The Dance of Anger.* New York: Harper & Row, 1985.

McFague, Sally. *The Body of God: An Ecological Theology.* Minneapolis: Fortress Press, 1993.

——. *Metaphorical Theology.* Philadelphia: Fortress Press, 1982.

Miller, Jean Baker. *Toward a Psychology of Women.* Boston: Beacon Press, 1976.

Mollenkott, Virginia Ramey. *The Divine Feminine.* New York: Crossroad, 1984.

——. *Sensuous Spirituality: Out from Fundamentalism.* New York: Crossroad, 1992.

Moltmann-Wendel, Elisabeth. *The Women Around Jesus,* trans. John Bowden. London: SCM Press, 1982.

Otwell, J.H. *And Sarah Laughed.* Philadelphia: The Westminster Press, 1977.

Pagels, Elaine. *The Gnostic Gospels.* New York: Random House, 1979.

Patai, Rafael. *The Hebrew Goddess.* Detroit: Wayne State University Press, 3rd ed., 1990.

Polanyi, Michael. *Personal Knowledge: Towards a Post-Critical Philosophy.* Chicago: The University of Chicago Press, 1958.

—— and Harry Prosch. *Meaning.* Chicago: The University of Chicago Press, 1975.

Random House Dictionary of the English Language, The, College Edition, ed. Laurence Urdang. New York: Random House, 1968.

Ricoeur, Paul. *The Rule of Metaphor: Multi-disciplinary Studies of the Creation of Meaning in Language,* trans. Robert Czerny. Toronto: University of Toronto Press, 1977.

Ridout, Godfrey. "My Song Is Love Unknown." *The Hymn Book of the Anglican Church of Canada and the United Church of Canada, 1971.*

Rodas, Ana Maria. *La Insurrection de Mariana.* Guatamala: Ediciones DEL CADEJO, 1993.

Rupp, Joyce. *The Star in My Heart: Experiencing Sophia, Inner Wisdom.* San Diego: LuraMedia, 1990.

Schmitt, Edward J. *Moving to Meaning: Some Issues in Planning Based on Parish Vision.* Edmonton: St. Stephen's College, 1988.

Schüssler Fiorenza, Elisabeth. *In Memory of Her.* New York: Crossroad, 1984.

Starhawk. *Dreaming the Dark: Magic, Sex & Politics.* Boston: Beacon Press, 1982.

Swidler, Leonard. *Biblical Affirmations of Woman.* Philadelphia: The Westminster Press, 1979.

Trible, Phyllis. *God and the Rhetoric of Sexuality.* Philadelphia: Fortress Press, 1978.

Weber, Kristin. *WomanChrist*. San Francisco: Harper & Row, 1987.

Wuellner, Flora Slosson. *Prayer and Our Bodies*. Nashville: The Upper Room, 1987.

Uhlein, Gabriele. *Meditations with Hildegard of Bingen*. Santa Fe: Bear & Co., 1982.

van Herk, Aritha. *Judith*. Toronto: McClellan and Stewart-Bantam Limited, 1978.

Index of Biblical References

— ✧ —